D1407699

From the library of

Starquest Expeditions 800-454-4149 www.starquestexpeditions.com

Dubrovnik

A CITY GUIDE

by

Annabel Barber

3rd edition

SOMERSET BOOKS

© 2006 Blue Guides Limited,
a Somerset Books company
editorial@blueguides.com
www.blueguides.com
Visible Cities is a registered trademark.

Layout & design: *Anikó Kuzmich, Regina Rácz*
Photographs: *Krešimir Strnad, Annabel Barber, Thomas Howells*
Ground plans & colour drawings: *Imre Bába*
Line drawings: *Michael Mansell RIBA*
Maps: *Dimap Bt.*

Acknowledgements:
*With special thanks to Milanka Bašić and Saša Bašić;
Also to Aida Cvjetković,
whose book* Dubrovačkim ulicama *has been an invaluable source.*

*Thanks also to the Dubrovnik Tourist Board, Dubrovnik Maritime
Museum, Mišo Ðuraš of Dubrovnik Museums, Pave Brailo, Mónika Hoffer,
Nada Marić, Sarah Marojica, Maya Mirsky, Mónika Papp,
Pero Pavlović, Žarko Ratković.
And to all those who have offered comments and suggestions on previous
editions, including: Tabitha Barber, Alan Becher,
Ann Ferdinand, Jean and Peter Hoare, Tom Ninkovich, Iskra Pavlović.*

This is the third edition of Visible Cities Dubrovnik:
corrections, comments and views will be welcomed.

Other titles in the Visible Cities series:
Visible Cities Barcelona
Visible Cities Budapest
Visible Cities Krakow
Visible Cities Vienna
Further titles are in preparation.

All rights reserved, including the right to
reproduce this book, or any portion thereof, in any form.

Cover illustration: *St Blaise, from a painting in the
Rector's Palace, Dubrovnik.*
Previous page: *Detail of Dubrovnik harbour, from an old print.*

ISBN 1-905131-15-1

5

CONTENTS

INTRODUCTION — 7
Pronunciation — 9
Ten things to do in Dubrovnik — 10
The story of St Blaise — 11

HISTORY — 13
Paying for peace — 13
The suzerainty of Venice — 14
Mediaeval empire building — 15
Ragusa's golden age — 16
The earthquake and its aftermath — 18
Napoleon and the end of the Republic — 19
Dubrovnik in the 19th century — 21
The 20th century — 21
A handful of dates — 23

MARITIME HISTORY — 25
The Dubrovnik fleet — 31

THE GOVERNMENT OF RAGUSA — 33

THE CITY WALLS — 39
Major fortifications — 41

MAJOR SIGHTS OF THE OLD TOWN — 45
The old port — 48
The Stradun — 51
The Rector's Palace — 57
The Sponza Palace — 66
The Franciscan friary — 68
The Dominican friary — 72
The church of St Blaise — 76
The cathedral — 78

ARCHITECTURE — 85
An overview of styles — 87
Major architects — 93

ART & MUSEUMS — 95
The Dubrovnik School — 96
Modern art — 98
Major museums — 100

RELIGIOUS MONUMENTS — 101
Churches & convents — 102
The synagogue and mosque — 106

GUIDED WALKS — 108
Walk One - *Around Od Pustijerne* — 111
Walk Two - *Around St Mary's* — 119
Walk Three - *Around Prijeko* — 127
Walk Four - *Ploče and beyond* — 134
Walk Five - *Pile and Brsalje* — 143

DAY TRIPS — 148
Lokrum — 150
The Elaphites — 155
Gruž & Rijeka Dubrovačka — 162
Zaton, Trsteno & Ston — 166
Cavtat — 170

PRACTICALITIES — 172
Food and wine — 173
Restaurants — 175
Cafés — 180
Food for picnics — 182
Hotels & accommodation — 183
Practical tips — 186

PART I
PART II
PART III
PART IV
PART V

BOXES	
St Blaise	11
Earthquakes	24
Tales from the sea	32
A handful of heroes	84
Literary Ragusans	132
Music in Ragusa	140

MAPS	
The Dalmatian littoral	6
Major sights	46
Ploče	134
Pile	142
The Elaphites	154
Restaurants & cafés	178
Dubrovnik old town	198

THE DALMATIAN LITTORAL

The hatched area is the territory
covered by the former Ragusan Republic.

INTRODUCTION

'This little land, which has been so ineffably blessed, whose inhabitants are gentle, hard-working and intelligent, an oasis of civilization in the midst of barbarism...' Thus enthused Alexandre Lauriston, the Napoleonic general who occupied Dubrovnik with his troops in 1806. His impressions still stand today. Dubrovnik is exquisitely beautiful—and though in itself it may be tranquil and peace-loving, its neighbours are decidedly volatile, a circumstance that Dubrovnik has suffered from greatly over the last decade, when the summer visitors on whom its survival so relies simply stayed away. Today let's hope that the dogs of war are firmly back in their kennels, and it is safe to enjoy Dubrovnik as an 'oasis of civilisation' again.

In its 15th and 16th-century heyday Dubrovnik was so famed as a centre of art and learning that it was dubbed the 'Croatian Athens'. This was due in part to its enormous dynamism: a small city state ready to accept Germans, Catalans, Greeks,

Dubrovnik old town, viewed from the south, gleaming white under a stormy sky.

Italians, Jews and Muslims—anyone, in fact, so long as they were hard-working, educated and entrepreneurial. Attracted by the promise of comfort and prosperity, people from the poorer hinterland also flocked to this land of milk and honey. And though the coveted prize of Dubrovnik citizenship was by no means automatically granted, physicians, engineers, scientists, craftsmen, artists, lawyers, cartographers, architects and seafarers were particularly welcome. Their legacy is the beautiful stone-built city that stands today, with all its monuments and its treasures.

The climate of Dubrovnik is typically Mediterranean: warm and sunny in the summer; cold, though hardly ever freezing, in the winter. The limestone bulk of Mt Srđ, which rises behind the town protects it in autumn and winter from the worst effects of the northerly Bora wind that whistles cruelly across the Dinaric Alps in the interior. Dubrovnik's vegetation is typically Mediterranean too, with groves of cypress, myrtle, oleander and pine. The name Dubrovnik is thought to derive from the native word for an oak forest, though the hillsides are not as wooded as they once were. Romans, Byzantines, Saracens, Venetians and Dubrovnik citizens themselves have all plundered them over the centuries for ship-building.

PRONUNCIATION

Croatian is a phonetic language, and provided you learn how to pronounce letters that either do not exist in English or which differ in their pronunciation from English, you should have no trouble:

c - 'ts', as in 'cats'

č - like the 'ch' in 'church'

ć - a softer version of č, more like the 'tue' in 'Tuesday'

đ - like the 'dg' in 'judge'; sometimes

this letter is written dj

g - always hard like the 'g' in 'game'

j - like the 'y' in 'yesterday'

š - like the 'sh' in 'ship'

ž - like the soft 'g' in 'garage'

Dubrovnik old harbour, protected by Fort St John and the Kaše wave-break, with the old quarantine hospital in the background.

TEN THINGS TO DO IN DUBROVNIK

1 Tour the city ramparts and enjoy unmatched vistas of the old town and surrounding sea (*p. 39*).

2 See the Rector's Palace, from where the ruling oligarchy governed the Republic for almost 500 years (*p. 57*).

3 Dine on today's catch, freshly grilled, with a view of the old port at Lokanda Peskarija (*p. 176*).

4 Meet the mariners and see the ships that made Dubrovnik great at the Maritime Museum (*p. 100*).

5 Bask on the sandy beach of Šunj on Lopud, the most beautiful of the Elaphite Islands (*p. 158*).

6 Find inner peace at the Franciscan friary, in Croatia's most beautiful mediaeval cloister (*p. 70*).

7 See two treasures of late mediaeval Ragusan art at the seaside nunnery of Dance (*p. 146*).

8 Stroll in Trsteno's sylvan glades, where Tasso, Titian and Byron all found inspiration (*p. 167*).

9 Drink chilled *prošek* on the terrace of the Gradska Kavana, overlooking the church of Dubrovnik's patron saint (*p. 181*).

10 Take a boat trip to Cavtat, site of the Graeco-Illyrian Epidaurum (*p. 170*).

DUBROVNIK OR RAGUSA?

Though the Slav name Dubrovnik was first recorded in 1189, the Latin derivation Ragusa was how the city was internationally known until the 20th century. In this book the two names are used interchangeably, though when referring to events that came after the fall of the Ragusan Republic in 1808, the name Dubrovnik is always used.

THE STORY OF ST BLAISE

Almost everywhere you go in Dubrovnik you are overlooked by the kindly figure of St Blaise: Sveti Vlaho. It was thanks to him, or so the legend goes, that Dubrovnik managed to defend herself against a Venetian attack in the 10th century. The Venetians' tactics were sly: they landed in Dubrovnik on the pretext of being en route for the Levant, and requested fresh water and supplies. But unbeknown to the Ragusans, they had left a sizeable fleet of gunships hidden half at Gruž and half at Lokrum. Just in time a Dubrovnik priest by the name of Stoico had a vision in which St Blaise appeared to him, warning that the Venetians were planning to mobilise their warships under cover of darkness. Stoico told the city authorities, who took the warning seriously, with the result that the citizens were armed and ready to repel the attack when it came.

So much for the legend. The historical Blaise was a bishop from 3rd-century Armenia, who was persecuted and martyred under the Roman governor Agricola. His relics came to Dubrovnik in 972, after which he was adopted as the patron saint of the city. The manner of Blaise's martyrdom is not certain, but some accounts say that he was flayed to death with iron combs, which is why a comb is often used as his emblem, and he has become the patron saint of woolcombers. He is also one of the Fourteen Holy Helpers, ancillary saints believed to be efficacious at curing human ailments. Blaise's ailment is sore throats, because his legend claims that he once saved a child from choking to death on a fish bone. There are people still living who remember placing their necks in the cleft between two crossed candles and praying to St Blaise to relieve their streptococcal infections. St Blaise's Day is celebrated on February 3rd (*see p. 186*). The day before that is Candlemas, when the candles are blessed.

Blaise is the symbol of the Dubrovnik Republic, his image appearing on the state flag, on Ragusan coins, over the gateways into the city, and impressed upon all the cannons that once bristled along the city walls.

HISTORY

The rocky outcrop on which the city of Dubrovnik stands was once an island, separated from the mainland by a marshy channel which oozed along the axis of the present-day Stradun. Evidence about the first inhabitants of the island is sketchy, but the remains of a 6th-century Byzantine church, discovered in the 1980s, seem to suggest that a largish community of Christian Illyrians lived here, one of a number of such communities scattered all the way up the Dalmatian coast, and ethnically separate from the pagan Slavic peoples who occupied the mountainous inland areas. The founders of the city that grew into modern Dubrovnik arrived around the middle of the 7th century, fleeing from the marauding Avars who had sacked the towns of Epidaurum (a Romanised Greek settlement on the site of today's Cavtat) and Salona. The refugees founded a new town, named Ragusium, which fell under the authority of the Byzantine Emperor, though it soon secured control of the whole of the surrounding area, as well as of the Elaphite Islands.

PAYING FOR PEACE

Dubrovnik's strategy for ensuring peaceful relations with her often turbulent neighbours, was usually simply to pay them money to go away. In around 878 the Byzantine Emperor Basil I decreed that Dalmatian towns should pay tribute to the Croatian and Slavonic rulers in order to secure peace, and Dubrovnik was one such town. This is the first instance of the slightly paradoxical-sounding custom of paying for prosperity that was to serve Dubrovnik well for the next thousand years.

The turn of the first millennium, the year 1000, saw an event which spelled the beginning of a long power struggle between the two greatest maritime powers in the region. Pietro Orseolo II, Doge of Venice, captured the whole of the Croatian Adriatic coast, and the people of Ragusa were compelled—at least for a time—to recognise his suzerainty. During the early mediaeval period, as Dubrovnik fell

St Blaise, from a painting by Nikola Božidarević, in the Dominican friary museum.

Coat of arms of the Ragusan Republic.

under the alternating suzerainty of Byzantium, Venice and the Normans, she began to demonstrate her true skill: bending the knee to powerful adversaries without allowing herself to be wholly subdued by them. And while she was happy to recognise the overall sovereignty of the shifting empires that battled for supremacy around her, she never—or hardly ever—surrendered her internal autonomy. Through an alliance with the Normans in the late 11th century she gained access to lucrative markets in southern Italy. As well as developing sea-borne commerce, she also had her eye on the regions inland. The late 12th century saw the start of a series of trade agreements with rulers from the hinterland, allowing Dubrovnik tax-free trading in Bosnia, the Byzantine Empire and Bulgaria. The Dubrovnik Commune also dates from this time. It is first mentioned in 1181, as a semi-autonomous proto-city state with an elected *Knez* (Rector) at its head.

THE SUZERAINTY OF VENICE

In 1202, in one of the most squalid episodes of mediaeval history, a Fourth Crusade was called. Ostensibly the aim was to attack Egypt, though this was nothing more than an excuse. In reality it was a series of plots and counter-plots by a jealous and greedy Holy Roman Emperor, intent on smashing the Eastern Christian Empire, allied with a grasping pretender to the throne of Byzantium and a corrupt and embittered old Doge, who had been blinded in Constantinople twenty-two years before, during a pogrom against Roman Catholics, and now had his sightless eyes fixed on revenge and spoils. Venice and the Catholic armies captured Constantinople in 1204, and the Frankish soldiers were given three days to ransack and ravage their fill. Nine hundred years of civilisation crumpled before the hooligan onslaught. Works of art that had survived from ancient Greece, masterpieces by local craftsmen, icons, church furnishings, libraries of sacred and learned texts were gleefully hacked to pieces by a drunken rabble. Men were murdered, children were mutilated, women were raped and left dying in the streets. Baldwin, Count of Flanders, was proclaimed Emperor, and the Venetians claimed almost half the city for themselves, plus other strategic territories in the western Aegean and Peloponnese. This left Dubrovnik extremely vulnerable. Byzantium was no longer able to offer her the protection that she had come to rely on, and Venice was quick to make her move, compelling Dubrovnik to recognise the sovereignty of the Doge, and installing a man of the Doge's choosing as Rector. He functioned as a kind of imperial proconsul, promising at his inauguration ceremony to respect local laws and customs, but essentially acting to promote Venetian interests. The battle for control of the seas became an uneven contest, with Venice showing no compunction about imposing punitive restrictions on Ragusan trade as well as taxing all goods except perishables that Ragusa sold in Venetian ports. But Venetian influence also had its positive side. Social and municipal development imitated the Venetian pattern, and ironically it was this that was ultimately to become one of the foundations of Dubrovnik's strength, eventually helping her to throw Venice off altogether. The Great Council, composed of the nobility, was set up, from which the Small Council and the Senate were elected. In 1272 came a comprehensive city statute regulating urban life and public hygiene, which remained essentially unchanged right up to the fall of the Ragusan Republic. And while Venice did much to cripple Dubrovnik's maritime activities, she did not prevent her from continuing to form alliances inland. Money exchanged hands and trade agreements were subsequently secured with part of Albania, all of Bulgaria, and Serbia, whose copper, iron, lead and silver were all exported through Dubrovnik.

MEDIAEVAL EMPIRE BUILDING

Dubrovnik also, albeit in a small way compared with most empire-builders, was busy acquiring strategic territories of her own. In the late 13th century the inhabitants of the island of Lastovo chose to join the Dubrovnik Commune, where they stayed until the year 1808. In 1333 Dubrovnik acquired a lease on Ston and

Pelješac, thus taking control of the important Ston salt works. About the same time, Dubrovnik began minting her own currency, and was to continue to do so until shortly before the final dissolution of the Ragusan Republic in 1808.

Towards the end of the 14th century, King Ostoja of Bosnia gave Dubrovnik a strip of land that effectively provided a link with her possessions on the Pelješac peninsula. In a fine example of mutual back-scratching, King Ostoja was made a Dubrovnik citizen, and was given a mansion in the town valued at 1500 ducats. Further expansion in the early 15th century took in the fertile Konavle valley and Cavtat. And with these acquisitions Ragusan expansion ended. At its height the Republic only comprised the narrow littoral from Ston in the north to just before the Bay of Kotor in the south, plus the offshore islands. The map on p. 6 shows the extent of the Republic's territory. One of the reasons so many subsequent empires were happy to do business with Dubrovnik was presumably because she was never a threat to their own territorial ambitions. She was a trader not a coloniser, and was more interested in commerce than conquest.

RAGUSA'S GOLDEN AGE

1358 is another key date for Ragusa, and as so often in her history, it denoted a change of allegiance. When King Louis I of Hungary expelled Venice from the eastern Adriatic, the Venetian threat receded once and for all. Dubrovnik renounced Venetian sovereignty, and acknowledged herself a dependent of the Kingdom of Hungary. As part of the oath of allegiance sworn to King Louis, Dubrovnik promised to pay an annual tribute of 500 ducats, sing lauds in the cathedral in the king's honour three times a year, as well as display the Hungarian flag and coat-of-arms and provide the king with a royal escort whenever he came to town. In return for all this the king promised to recognise Ragusan control of certain inland and coastal territories. Dubrovnik was allowed to trade with Venice and Serbia, even when Hungary was at war with them. Dubrovnik's population at this time was a hybrid mixture of Slavs, Greeks, Jews, Catalans, Italians and Germans, all speaking a local Latin-based language, which survived until the 16th century. Though the Slav element of the population was by now almost the majority, Dubrovnik as yet felt no particular leaning towards Croatia (at that time part of the Kingdom of Hungary), and no desire to be strongly linked to her. For this reason she tried to keep her agreement with

View of Dubrovnik before the earthquake of 1667, from a painting in the Franciscan friary museum. Note the arcaded palaces along the Stradun.

Hungary as loose as possible, while still managing to ensure that the alliance paved the way for burgeoning prosperity and genuine autonomy, as well as providing access to a number of inland markets controlled by King Louis. The Ragusan nobles once again began to elect their Rector from their own ranks. Thus the native aristocracy took over the rule of the town, and though a later aspirant to the Hungarian throne, Ladislas of Naples, sold his claims on Dalmatia to Venice, Venice never managed to subordinate Ragusa again. Dubrovnik's greatest era had begun.

The end of the 14th century also saw Ragusa's first agreement with a country that was to become crucial to her future prosperity. The Ottoman Sultan, Sarhan, granted Dubrovnik free trade on Turkish soil. The relationship was an uneasy one at first, however, and as the Ottoman empire began to creep steadily westwards, Dubrovnik appealed to the Pope and to the King of Hungary to join forces to stop the infidel advance. Much good it did her—the Turks crushed the Hungarians at Varna and moved inexorably further into Europe. Dubrovnik's reaction to the situation was to re-think the expediency of her alliance with

Hungary: by 1481 she was trading freely in Ottoman territory in return for an annual tribute of 12,500 ducats. When in 1526 the Ottoman armies resoundingly defeated Hungary at the Battle of Mohács, Dubrovnik was swift to take advantage of her contacts with Turkey and recognise the sovereignty of the Sultan, under whose formal protection she remained until the dissolution of the Ragusan Republic. During the subsequent Christian wars against Turkish dominion Dubrovnik, having vital interests in both camps, remained neutral—with dramatic results in terms of her trade, which boomed. The 15th and 16th centuries were unquestionably Dubrovnik's golden age. Though the Republic's total population stood at only around 35,000, in terms of cargo capacity her merchant fleet ranked third in the world. And her ruling families were spending their enormous wealth on architecture and paintings, building themselves lavish palaces, furnishing them sumptuously, and extending patronage to all branches of the arts.

THE EARTHQUAKE & ITS AFTERMATH

By the early 17th century, however, this seemingly boundless prosperity was already on the wane. Dubrovnik's role as entrepôt was no longer worth what it had been, as the high seas were increasingly dominated by England and Holland, and the Mediterranean was being reduced to something of a backwater. The beginning of the end came in 1667, when Dubrovnik was devastated by an earthquake. Around 4,000 citizens—about half the population of the city—were killed (*see p. 24*). And though the city was rebuilt, it was in nothing like the grand style of before the disaster. A solid, harmonious white stone town emerged, but most of the extravagant Renaissance palaces were gone for ever. It was the first definitive step on the path to final decline.

A mere couple of decades later Dubrovnik found herself having to make urgent strategic plans. The Turks were defeated at the gates of Vienna in 1683, and expelled from the Hungarian capital Buda in 1686. Eugene of Savoy and the united Christian armies had begun implacably rolling them back eastwards. Venice took advantage of the turmoil to pounce on Dubrovnik, capture a part of her inland territory and begin to attack her borders, threatening to cut off access to her inland trade routes. In view of this danger, Dubrovnik chose another ally. Knowing that hard-pressed Turkey could not be relied on, and that she would

'Libertas', the symbolic personification of Dubrovnik, beset by Venice on one side and Turkey on the other. Relief from the base of the statue of the poet Gundulić.

probably lose Bosnia and Herzegovina to the armies of Prince Eugene, Dubrovnik sent emissaries to the Holy Roman Emperor Leopold in Vienna. Harking back to the old Ragusan-Hungarian pact of 1358, Dubrovnik accepted Austrian sovereignty in return for an annual tribute of 500 ducats. At the same time she kept her options open by continuing to recognise the sovereignty of Turkey; a typically Ragusan policy of keeping more than one horse in the race.

NAPOLEON BONAPARTE & THE END OF THE RAGUSAN REPUBLIC

But Austria was not as complaisant an overlord as Hungary or Turkey had been. When in 1765 Dubrovnik wanted to open a consulate in Zagreb (she already had consulates in Paris and Rome), the move was vetoed by Vienna. Ragusa was losing her power. When the might of her great adversary Venice finally collapsed forever in 1797, quivering before the conquering might of Napoleon, Dubrovnik felt the trade benefits only for a few short years. Less than a decade later, in

Clocks in the Rector's Palace were once set at a quarter to six, allegedly the fateful hour when Napoleon's men entered the city in 1806. The tradition was picturesque, but it seems to have lost favour.

1806, Dubrovnik found herself caught in the middle of a tussle between France and Russia. She made urgent appeals to both sides, as well as to Austria and Turkey, but it was to no avail. France and Russia both wanted to possess Dubrovnik, and the city's leaders found themselves in an entirely unfamiliar situation: their time-honoured scheme of playing one adversary off against another wasn't working, and the Senate had no idea whether to place its future in French hands or Russian. In the end they opted for France, with the result that Dubrovnik was occupied by foreign troops for the first time in her history. In 1808 Napoleon appointed his marshal, General Marmont, Duc de Raguse; the Ragusan Republic was abolished, and all its territories were placed under French control. Reluctantly the Senate had to acknowledge defeat. A year later, in 1809, Dubrovnik was made part of Napoleon's Illyrian Provinces, remaining there until Bonaparte's own star began to tumble. At the Congress of Vienna, following Napoleon's ultimate defeat at the hands of Wellington and Blücher, Dubrovnik was integrated into the Kingdom of Dalmatia and annexed to Austria-Hungary, where she remained until 1918.

DUBROVNIK IN THE NINETEENTH CENTURY

Dubrovnik's history is inextricably bound up with Croatia's after this. 1848, the great year of anti-Habsburg revolutions, saw Croatia following the trend. Discovering a sense of ethnic identity, romantic young nationalists began demanding the unification of Dalmatia and Croatia, and the inclusion of the new province into the greater Slavic brotherhood. 1849 saw the first publication of the periodical *Dubrovnik, Flower of National Literature* (*Dubrovnik, cvijet narodnog knjizevstva*), in which the ardent Pan-Slavist Petar Preradović published his famous poem *To Dubrovnik*. Ragusan breasts were inflamed with the idea of Southern Slavic identity. Dubrovnik replaced Ragusa as the city appellation of choice, and strenuous efforts were made to introduce the Croatian language into schools and offices, and to promote Croatian-language books. The conservative-minded Emperor Franz Joseph had been troubled by enough of that sort of thing in neighbouring Hungary, however. The last thing he wanted was a united phalanx of Slavs at his empire's throat. He responded by passing a decree prohibiting the unification of Dalmatia and Croatia and outlawing any further political activity with this end in view.

The People's Party, the champions of unification, nevertheless remained very strong in Dubrovnik. Being an outpost had been all very well in the days of merchant prosperity; now it felt distinctly precarious, particularly with the Ottoman frontier only a matter of miles away, a mere two hours' walk from the old town. Dubrovnik was extremely keen to cement her ties with Croatia. But Austria was obdurate. The people had to put their hopes on hold, and concentrate on creating a new kind of prosperity. Factories were built to manufacture soap, oil and pasta, ceramics, candles and tobacco. Unification was not in fact achieved until Austria-Hungary itself had collapsed after the end of the First World War.

WARS & RENEWAL: THE TWENTIETH CENTURY

In 1918 Dubrovnik, with Dalmatia and Croatia, was incorporated into the new Kingdom of Serbs, Croats and Slovenes, partly thanks to the offices of the politician Frano Supilo, a great champion of Croato-Serb cooperation. In 1929 this became the Kingdom of Yugoslavia. These were not happy years for

Dubrovnik, however. They were times of recession and hardship throughout Dalmatia, and saw a tidal wave of emigrations, mainly to the United States, as the hungry populace sought their daily bread elsewhere. The result of this was a groundswell of support for the Communist Party (in the elections to the Constituent Assembly in 1920, the Communists received an outright majority in the Dubrovnik area). Though the party was outlawed a year later, this did not prevent furtive support for Communist activity behind the scenes.

After the outbreak of World War Two, the ruling Karađorđević family tried to keep Yugoslavia out of hostilities, hoping that the Allies would take control of the Mediterranean and thus offer his country protection. Italy's entry into the war in 1940, on the side of the Axis powers, dashed all Yugoslavia's hopes. Albania fell to Italy, Austria was controlled by the Nazis, Hungary, Bulgaria and Romania all had Axis sympathies (at least until Romania changed sides in 1944)—Yugoslavia found herself surrounded. When the German attack on the country inevitably began, Russia reneged on the Treaty of Friendship she had recently signed with King Paul, and announced that Yugoslavia no longer existed. The country was partitioned and a separate state of Croatia was formed, which included Dubrovnik. It was a state in name only, however: Italian forces had entered Dubrovnik in April 1941, and continued to control the city until Italy's capitulation in 1943, after which the city fell to the Germans. Resistance came from AVNOJ, the Anti-Fascist Council for the National Liberation of Yugoslavia, a movement whose Communist Partisans were increasingly seen by Churchill as the only effective force against Axis occupation. By December Churchill and Roosevelt had joined with Stalin in agreeing to support them, even though this would inevitably mean a Communist future for Yugoslavia after the war was over. In the autumn of 1944 Dubrovnik was liberated (not without considerable bloodshed) by units of the Dalmatian Brigade of the People's Liberation Army, and when the war ended she became part of the Republic of Croatia, a semi-autonomous unit within Federal Yugoslavia, under Tito.

And here she remained until the final collapse of Communism. In 1991 a referendum was held, and in the Dubrovnik area 94% of the voters voted for a sovereign Croatian state. With Serbia pushing for a unified Yugoslavia, however, and the United States refusing to recognise Croatian independence, the situation escalated into armed conflict. The Yugoslav army began its attack on Dubrovnik on October 1st, destroying the port of Gruž and the airport at Čilipi, and shelling targets inside the old city walls. It was partly this destruction of one of the world's cherished historic sites, reported extensively in the international press, that led the tide of support for Serbia to ebb so dramatically. Germany, followed by the EU as a whole, decided to recognise Croatia's independence, and Dubrovnik was eventually freed in the latter part of 1992. Serbian forces had never managed to penetrate the old town, and, though their mortar attacks had caused much damage and a number of buildings had caught fire, the scale of the destruction was mercifully not as great as the world had feared. This is not to downplay what the town and its people suffered, and the old city stonework still visibly bears its scars, but thankfully most of Dubrovnik's monuments are still there to be enjoyed.

A HANDFUL OF DATES

667 *First written record of the name (Ragusium).*

1181 *First mention of the Dubrovnik Commune, seed of the future city state.*

1358 *Dubrovnik finally breaks away from the sovereignty of Venice, and comes under Hungarian protection.*

1526 *Dubrovnik seeks Turkish protection.*

1667 *Dubrovnik devastated by the Great Earthquake.*

1808 *Napoleon abolishes the Ragusan Republic.*

1815 *Dubrovnik annexed to Austria following the Congress of Vienna.*

1918 *Dubrovnik becomes part of Croatia in the Kingdom of Serbs, Croats and Slovenes.*

1991–92 *The Siege of Dubrovnik.*

1992 *Croatia's status as an independent republic receives international recognition.*

EARTHQUAKES

Three major earthquakes have afflicted Dubrovnik during her long history. The first came in 1520. The most recent was in 1979, and much of the destruction that it caused is still visible today, on the seaward side of the old town, south of the Stradun. By far the most famous earthquake, however, was the Great Quake that rocked the city in the 17th century.

About two hours after sunrise, on April 6th 1667, when most of the population was still in bed or at least indoors, an earthquake lasting fifteen seconds shook the city to its foundations. According to the poet Giacomo Pamotta, who wrote about the incident afterwards, almost every building was destroyed, or if not destroyed then badly damaged. Among the casualties were the Rector himself and several members of the Senate. For days all the pupils from a boys' school were heard under the rubble, calling for aid. People were so frantic to escape that they did not bother to extinguish the fires which had broken out all over town, and gusty winds helped these to spread, while Bosnian traders who had come for the market looted and pillaged. Nor was it only the Bosnians who looted. Poorer Ragusans cheerfully stripped rings and gold buttons from victims trapped in the rubble, often refusing to pull people free unless they could offer some booty. When the worst of the commotion had died down, the town was quickly rebuilt, though not in the grand Renaissance style of before the disaster. Chroniclers have claimed that this was a gesture of generosity: that the nobles decided not to make their palaces too ostentatious so as not to lord it over their traumatised people. That may be the complexion they placed on things; the reality probably had more to do with shortage of money.

MARITIME HISTORY

'Argosies with portly sail, the pageants of the sea'. So Shakespeare describes them in *The Merchant of Venice*, those characteristic chubby wooden freighter ships that plied the Mediterranean in their heyday of the 15th and 16th centuries. The word argosy is derived directly from the word Ragusa. Used initially to describe the Ragusan carrack, the largest type of cargo ship of Ragusan origin, it came in time to denote any ship of a similar type, even if the ship was not, in the words of the partisan Ragusan Nikola Sagroević, 'the strongest in the world and made from the finest wood'.

By the late 16th century, the largest of the Ragusan argosies were four-masted floating monoliths, capable of carrying 100 tons and manned by 140 crew (captain, officers and sailors, along with smiths, carpenters, cannoneers, a doctor and a clerk). Each ship had its own carpentry, smithy, supply of drinking water,

Mid-16th-century three-masted Dubrovnik galleon, the second largest type of vessel in the fleet after the carrack.

plus a styful of live pigs, a rabbit hutch, and a hen-coop with enough chickens to feed the crew. 'If she only manages to complete one or two voyages, she can pay back all the money invested in her,' as the reckoning went. And some of these vessels lasted an amazing thirty years.

By virtue of her very position, jutting precariously into the sea, Dubrovnik was forced to master the art of seafaring early in her history, and to make a virtue out of sheer necessity. In the mid-9th century a Saracen sea raid which lasted over a year left the hard-pressed citizens with no option but to call on the Byzantine Emperor to send aid. But it was not long before Dubrovnik had learned to look after herself, and just two years after this incident she was using her own ships to transport Croatian soldiers to help oust the Saracens from Bari. A tiny city like Dubrovnik could not be expected to survive entirely alone, however; one of Ragusa's greatest sources of strength was her wiliness over whom to form alliances with, and what terms to demand when drawing up the contract.

In 1081 Dubrovnik allied herself with the Norman navy in a battle against her old protector, Byzantium, and her lifelong sparring partner and fellow maritime power, Venice. From a strategic point of view it had been a clever move. For the next five years Dubrovnik recognised the nominal sovereignty of the Normans in return for help in penetrating the lucrative markets of southern Italy and Sicily. Soon commercial interests became the driving force behind Ragusan development, and she found herself using her navy less for battle than as a tool for amassing new business, concluding treaties with towns up and down the Dalmatian and Italian coasts. The 12th century saw trade agreements negotiated with Molfetta, Pisa, Ravenna and Ancona; the early 13th century added to these the towns of Bari, Ferrara, Rimini and Epirus. Dubrovnik traded in textiles, wood, cattle, leather, wool, grain, wax, wine, slaves (though the slave trade was abolished in 1416), metal ores, hunting birds, salt, gold and gold artifacts. Her status as a major trading centre was assured and her future entrepôt status between inland regions to the east and western lands over the sea began to take shape.

But Venice always remained a force to be reckoned with, and the 13th century was a particularly turbulent time, with Venice alternately forcing Dubrovnik to acknowledge the authority of the Doge and abide by swingeing trade restrictions, and having to rescind these restrictions when Dubrovnik threw the Doge out of town. Unwilling to continue this game of cat and mouse

Square-sailed Dubrovnik brigantine flying the flag of St Blaise.

forever, the merchants of Dubrovnik began to channel their trade overland away from sea routes, so as not to be quite so much at Venice's mercy. In 1358, however, the turning point came. The Hungarian King, Louis I, who also controlled Croatia, expelled Venice from the eastern Adriatic. Dubrovnik seized her chance, swearing an oath of allegiance to the Hungarian crown which was to gain her a powerful protector for almost the next two hundred years. According to the terms of the oath, Dubrovnik was obliged to send her fleet to assist Hungary in any conflict involving a Dalmatian town. Dubrovnik thus had to build a fleet of suitable deterrent power, and costly though that was, it also laid the foundation for her great maritime supremacy. Ragusan shipbuilders became famous, and the Republic learned to guard them jealously, refusing to let them work for any other state or government.

A couple of decades later, in 1373, another trade breakthrough was achieved when Pope Gregory XI granted a special dispensation allowing Dubrovnik to trade with 'infidels'—she was the first Christian power to be accorded this privilege. Later still, in 1433, Sigismund of Hungary obtained a special *privilegium navigationis ad partes Orientis* for Dubrovnik, allowing her to trade in all non-Christian countries, to transport pilgrims and goods to the Holy Land, and to build churches and establish consulates in Islamic countries. The privilege gave Dubrovnik almost exclusive rights to trade with the Turks, which in turn led to enormous profit, as well as laying the foundation stone for the next strategic alliance of the future.

The 16th century was Dubrovnik's maritime golden age. She owned more ships than ever before: ocean-going carracks and galleons, and smaller coastal vessels for navigation within the Adriatic, in all employing some 5,000 sailors, about a seventh of the Republic's total population. In the first part of the 16th century, before England began to flex her maritime muscle, Dubrovnik's fleet of ocean-going vessels was third in the world after Spain and the Netherlands, and her shipwrights said to be second in skill only to the Portuguese. In 1507 Dubrovnik placed herself under the protection of Spain, then the mightiest ruler in the western world. This opportune alliance meant that Dubrovnik was able to carry on uninterrupted trade throughout the whole of the central and western Mediterranean, and to develop her trade outside that area too. The relationship with Spain was not entirely rosy, however. In 1535 the Spanish King and Holy Roman Emperor, Charles V, mounted an attack on Tunis, in which the Ragusan navy was persuaded to take part. It lost fifteen of its best galleons. Three years later came the first war between the Holy League of Spain, Venice and Austria against Ottoman Turkey. Venice attempted to involve Dubrovnik in the war on the side of Christendom, but Dubrovnik had learned caution. Not only this; since the mid-15th century she had enjoyed highly favourable trade privileges from the Turkish Sultan, and in 1526, when the Ottoman army had routed the Hungarians at the Battle of Mohács, Dubrovnik had cut her losses, abandoned her agreement with Hungary, and recognised Turkish suzerainty instead. By cleverly maintaining her neutrality during this conflict, therefore, she managed to increase her trade by three or four times what it had been in peacetime. At the Battle of Lepanto in the year 1571, the Dubrovnik navy, again keen to preserve its neutrality, did not directly take part, although her warships were standing by on the side of the Holy League. In 1588, however, Dubrovnik lost her head. Hoping to profit from the expansion of Spanish Atlantic trade routes, Ragusan ships joined forces with the 'Invincible Armada' of Philip II, in its doomed raid on England. England retaliated by expelling all Dubrovnik traders from her shores—and trade with Britain was not resumed until 1759.

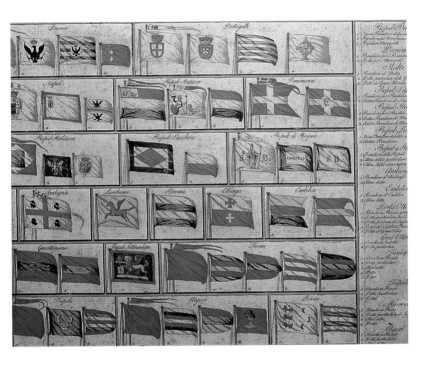

Three flags of the Ragusan Republic are shown on the outer right hand side, third row from the top.

Strained relations with England were not the only problem. In the final years of the 16th century Venice had built a warehouse in Split, further up the Dalmatian coast. Dubrovnik, which until then had been the main Dalmatian intermediary for trade between east and west, found that the caravans were starting to bypass her and and re-route to Split. Dubrovnik tried to cast around for other markets, but it was increasingly difficult. The great trading companies of England and Holland now controlled the high seas; oceanic routes were being opened up, and the Mediterranean was turning into a *cul-de-sac*. Attempts by Venice to paralyse Dubrovnik's trade on the mainland did not help matters; nor did the fact that throughout the century things went very badly for Dubrovnik's great protector, Turkey, in a succession of wars with Austria and Venice. In the 18th century, though, things began to improve. By sticking to her policy of dogged neutrality, Dubrovnik prospered as a carrier of other nations' goods.

When almost everyone else in Europe entered the Napoleonic débacle, Dubrovnik must have thought her fortunes had well and truly turned: for a brief few years after the fall of Venice in 1797 she enjoyed what was effectively a carrying monopoly. But it wasn't to last. Napoleon took a dim view of her professed neutrality, accused her of colluding with Russia, and sent his troops to occupy the town in 1806. Two years later he dissolved the Ragusan Republic. Dubrovnik's glory days were over.

Brave attempts were made to restore them. The natural harbour of Gruž, capable of taking vessels of larger draught, became the main port of the town. In 1875 the *Dubrovnik Twelfth* was launched, one of the largest ships in the Adriatic at the time, and the Emperor Franz Joseph came down from Vienna to see her off on her maiden voyage. But when Dubrovnik came to make the switch from sail power to steam five years later, she found herself purchasing her ships rather than building them. And in any case, pottering about in the Mediterranean was not really enough—already by the 17th century its deficiencies had become apparent. To say that between the two world wars Gruž was the second most important port in Yugoslavia is not saying much for a city that had been

The launching of the Dubrovnik Twelfth *in Gruž harbour in 1875.*

accustomed to being first in the known world. The founding of the Transatlantic shipping company Atlantska Plovidba in 1956 gave something of a fillip to Dubrovnik's dwindling maritime fortunes, it is true. When in 1991 plans were announced to create a marina in Gruž, however, it was clear that the transformation of Dubrovnik from trading ground to pleasure ground was going full steam ahead.

THE DUBROVNIK FLEET

In its late 16th-century heyday, the Ragusan fleet had around 180 ships and a total freight capacity of 700,000 hectolitres (the equivalent of a hundred million bottles of wine). Ships were, from the smallest to the largest:

THE SAGITTA (Literally 'arrow'): light and speedy, often used as passenger or fishing craft;

THE CARAVEL: Fast trading boat for carrying light cargoes;

THE BRIGANTINE: Two or three-masted, square-rigged merchantman;

THE GALLEON: Three-masted trading vessel with raised decks fore and aft;

THE CARRACK: Three or four-masted merchant ship and man-of-war, with a tonnage of over 2,000 hectolitres.

Tales from the Sea

The Legend of Sveti Andrija

Many centuries ago, on the island of Lopud, there lived a beautiful girl named Maria. Maria was an orphan, and kept house for her two brothers, both of them humble fishermen. One day a handsome nobleman was shipwrecked in the bay where their cottage stood. Maria took him in, gave him dry clothes and a bed for the night. The two fell hopelessly in love, but it was a doomed passion. In the days of the Ragusan Republic marriage between a noble and a commoner could scarcely be countenanced. Rather than marry another, the nobleman retired to the monastery on the remote island of Sv. Andrija. Every night he would come down to the shore with a lantern and light the way for Maria to swim out to meet him. In time her brothers found out, and were horrified that the family was being so dishonoured. They waited until Maria set out on her nightly swim, and put out to sea in their fishing boat, lighting a lamp, which Maria mistook for her lover's signal. On and on she swam, with her brothers guiding her ever further out of her way. At last she could swim no more and was subsumed by the waves.

Some Famous Men of the Sea

Ivo Raçić's schooner Petka.

TOMO & VICE SKOÇIBUHA: Tomo & Vice were father and son, wealthy shipowners and patrons of the arts from the island of Šipan. Their turreted summer residence on Šipan survives, in the harbour village of Suđurađ. In Dubrovnik old town is the family's magnificent, crumbling mid-16th-century Renaissance palace (*see pp. 114–15*).

IVO RAČIĆ: Račić was an enterprising shipowner from Cavtat. Though originally his ships sailed mainly in Mediterranean waters, he spotted the way maritime fortunes were turning in the 19th century, and founded the Račić Transatlantic Company, with fourteen ocean-going liners. He is commemorated by a glorious semi-pagan mausoleum above Cavtat harbour, the work of sculptor Ivan Meštrović (*see p. 171*).

MIHO PRACAT: Pracat was a shipowner and merchant-adventurer from the island of Lopud. When he died without an heir, in 1607, he left the whole of his enormous fortune to the Ragusan Republic. He is honoured with a bust in the atrium of the Rector's Palace.

THE GOVERNMENT
OF RAGUSA

The peoples of the Adriatic shore are the heirs of all the civilisations that once flourished in the Mediterranean—the Greeks, the Minoans, the Illyrians, the Phoenicians, the Romans and many others besides. Each has left monuments and some half-hidden racial traits, which appear quite unexpectedly and account perhaps for the great beauty of the women in the villages near Dubrovnik.' So wrote a fulsome Eric Whelpton in the 1950s. But there is another theory about this mysterious great beauty, too. The story goes that when Dubrovnik came under Austrian control, in 1815, its ruling class vowed to stop marrying, claiming that they would rather become extinct than live under alien rule. What they meant by extinction, in fact, was legitimate extinction. The urge to procreate was much

'Forget private concerns; think of the public good.' Exhortation to the governors of Dubrovnik on the entrance to the former Great Council chambers in the Rector's Palace.

too strong to be withstood, and affairs between noblemen and peasant girls from the surrounding villages flourished. The result? A breed of pedigree noble savages that Rousseau would have drooled over, but none of them entitled to their father's inheritance. The old family names have died out, and there is not a single legitimate descendant of the old Ragusan nobles now alive. Their voluntary programme of self-extermination was an unqualified success, and the last true-born Ragusan aristocrat is reputed to have died not long after the Second World War.

Dubrovnik has never had a monarch. In the earliest days it was governed jointly by a council of nobles and a People's Assembly, but gradually the people ceased to be consulted, and government passed into the hands of the aristocracy, turning the state into an oligarchy along Venetian lines. In 1358, when Dubrovnik at last threw off Venetian control forever, the Ragusan Commune began to style itself a republic. It was governed by its Great Council, a body which consisted of all male nobles over the age of 18. This council elected the Senate, whose 45 members, re-elected annually, controlled all foreign and domestic policy. There was also an executive body, the Small Council, consisting of 11 members with a one-year term of office.

The titular head of government was the Rector, a figure who enjoyed plenty of pomp and ceremony but little real power. With the governance of the little republic resting in the hands of so few families, all the nobility was concerned to limit the personal power of individuals, lest a Julius Caesar should suddenly rise from their midst and demand a crown. The Rector changed every month, and the same man could only be re-elected after a lapse of two years. During his rectorship he was more or less confined to his palace.

The Ragusan aristocrats were a different breed—literally—from their subjects. The nobles were descendants of those first Romano-Illyrian settlers who colonised the rocky headland back in the 7th century. By the Republic's heyday the majority of the population was of Slavic origin—and though of course the nobles had intermarried with Slavic families, they still retained an aura of difference. They spoke Italian, and their names were Italian, though there was a vernacular version of each name too: Gondola/Gundulić; Bona/Bunić. They tended to send their sons abroad for their education, either to Italian universities, or to Salamanca and the Sorbonne, and on their return those sons were expected to marry a Ragusan nobleman's daughter. Anyone who married a commoner would automatically forfeit his birthright. In our egalitarian age it is easy to sneer or to portray these people as inbred fools—but the organism they created by their system of

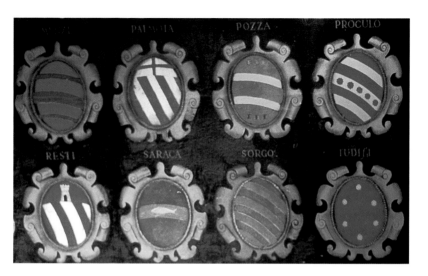

Coats of arms of the Ragusan nobility, from an illuminated panel in the Rector's Palace.

governance survived and prospered in a notoriously turbulent region for almost half a millennium, which is no mean feat.

During the golden age of the Republic the nobles ruled more or less un-opposed, and none of the wealthy shipowners or merchants seems to have minded his lesser status. It was impossible for a commoner to be ennobled—or at least to receive a hereditary title—and no commoner seems particularly to have desired it. After all, a merchant could make far more money than a noble; a title would just be the icing on an already very rich cake. After the Great Earthquake of 1667, however, things changed. The death toll had been so great that the patrician families found themselves in danger of dying out altogether, so the Great Council decided to admit ten new families into the ranks of the aristocracy, accepting a further five families a few years later. The old nobles and the new creations found it difficult to see eye to eye, and it was not long before an intense rivalry sprang up between the Salamancan-educated (who were generally considered to be hidebound and conservative), and the Sorbonne-educated (who were considered—or more probably considered themselves—to be liberal and free-thinking). The two factions refused to intermarry, and cut all social contact except for what was unavoidable at official functions. The squabbling in the upper echelons of society began to infuriate the middle classes. And there was another cause for discontent, too. Dubrovnik's boomtime was over. In the past its merchants had amassed huge fortunes. Men like Vice Skočibuha (*pictured right*) were able to afford a lifestyle equivalent to that of any noble, if not more opulent still. Now increasing international competition and a weakened Ottoman empire meant that things were a little tighter. Perceiving the ruling elite to be at fault and ineffectual, many of the wealthier burghers began to resent having no say in how their Republic was governed. Soon they began to agitate for more power.

The nobles remained for the most part unmoved, continuing to make it very difficult for parvenus to be ennobled, and also curtailing the influence of the wealthy middle classes by preventing many of them from purchasing land. This inflexible attitude meant that the Great Council, which had had around 300 members in the 16th century, had dwindled to a mere 70 members by the 18th. It also

Vice Skočibuha (d. 1588), the wealthy shipowner and merchant from the island of Šipan, who turned down the chance to be ennobled when he found it would not be a hereditary title.

meant that the middle classes, antagonised by their rulers, had begun to think the unthinkable: maybe the precious independence of the Dubrovnik Republic didn't count for so much after all; maybe they would be better off under someone else. When the French eventually occupied the town, many families welcomed them, and when Napoleon dissolved the Senate, the bourgeois worthies gave a ball to celebrate the demise of oligarchy. The taxes that the French levied and the system of conscription that they introduced soured the euphoria somewhat, though, and it wasn't long before the nobles were trying to stage a comeback, with their citizens' blessing. But Napoleon had no time for such plots. He arrested the ringleaders and threatened to have them shot unless they came to heel. For a time everything went quiet. Then, when Napoleon finally fell, the nobles tried to restore their Republic once again. It was a doomed attempt. None of the European powers seemed interested in supporting the Ragusan cause, and Austria stepped in vigorously to remind everyone that she had been awarded control of the region at the Congress of Vienna. It was then, acknowledging that all was lost, that the Dubrovnik nobles made their dramatic and supremely romantic gesture, electing simply to become extinct.

PART II

GUIDE TO THE CITY

p. 39   THE CITY WALLS

p. 45   MAJOR SIGHTS OF THE OLD TOWN
The old port - p. 48
The Stradun - p. 51
The Rector's Palace - p. 57
The Sponza Palace - p. 66
The Franciscan friary - p. 68
The Dominican friary - p. 72
The church of St Blaise - p. 76
The cathedral - p. 78

p. 85   ARCHITECTURE
Historical overview - p. 87
Major architects - p. 93

p. 95   ART & MUSEUMS
The Dubrovnik School - p. 96
Modern art - p. 98
Major museums - p. 100

p. 101   RELIGIOUS MONUMENTS
Churches and convents - p. 102
The synagogue and mosque - p. 106

THE CITY WALLS

High on a crag above the western edge of the old town broods the austere and sombre Fort Lovrijenac. Carved above its entrance is a Latin motto which, loosely translated, reads 'Liberty is not for sale, not even for gold'. Proud words—and for the four and a half centuries that she remained a free trading republic, Dubrovnik was able to live up to them, happily sacrificing any number of ducats in exchange for her precious autonomy. Her fabled skill in diplomacy was one thing that made this possible; the other was the calm impregnability of her fortifications.

The first circlet of walls was built in the 8th century, around the Latin town of Ragusium, protecting it from the landward Slavs and seaward Saracens. Gradually, as the city expanded outwards, so too did the walls. The unbroken ring of bastioned fortifications that survives today is largely the result of plans

The old city of Dubrovnik, safely encircled within her protective stone girder. The island of Lokrum can be seen in the background.

drawn up in the 15th century by the Republic's official engineer Pasko Miličević. Constantinople had fallen to the Turks in 1453, and alarmed by the prospect of an Ottoman advance, Ragusa decided to strengthen her defences. Built of great blocks of stone, the walls are almost two kilometres in total length, and in some places up to 25 metres high and six metres wide. They are reinforced with bastions along the long sides and stout forts at the corners. Two free-standing defences complete the system: Fort Lovrijenac to the west, and the Revelin to the east. The walls are pierced by five gates. Two of these lead directly from the old port: Vrata Ribarnice (Fishmarket Gate), which takes you into the top of the Stradun; and Vrata od Ponte (Harbour Gate), which takes you out alongside the Rector's Palace, opposite the cathedral. The other gates are road gates: Pile to the west, Ploče to the east, and Buža to the north. Above these gates, as well as on the seaward bastions, stands the effigy of St. Blaise, patron of the city (*see p. 11*), keeping watch for suspect intruders.

Alas, he was of little use against the French—perhaps because they did not arrive with cannons and gunships, but spoke with distinctly forked tongue. The Ragusan writer Ivo Vojnović once complained that Dubrovnik's problem was precisely that she could not cut loose from her walls. They protected her in times of obvious aggression, but against a subtler enemy they were useless, binding her fast, preventing her from slashing her moorings and floating out to sea out of harm's way.

On 26th May 1806, General Alexandre Lauriston, commander of Napoleon's army, coolly knocked on the main city gate and requested admittance. Two senators read out a formal protest, but with Russian warships infesting the Mediterranean at the time, the Ragusans knew that they had to choose between the deep blue sea and the devil: the gates were duly opened and the French permitted to enter. Lauriston insisted that he and his men were merely passing through, promising to evacuate Dubrovnik as soon as peace was achieved between France and Russia. Napoleon, however, had other ideas. He wrote to Beauharnais that he had no intention of evacuating the city, and that in fact he fully intended to take it over and organise its affairs. The French troops stayed for two years. In January 1808 the Tricolore was hoisted from Orlando's column, and the Senate of Ragusa was declared to have been dissolved. The Republic, Ragusa was told, no longer existed. In March Napoleon gave the title Duc de Raguse to his marshal, Auguste Frédéric Marmont. The famous walls had never been attacked, so how could they have been used to defend? Within a very short time Napoleon's men had built something which put those proud walls to shame: Fort Imperial, towering over the city from the heights of Mount Srđ: an edifice designed simultaneously to protect and to subjugate.

Today the city walls function as a sort of aerial promenade, and the best way to enjoy them is to walk their entire length, admiring the chequered roofscape, the views out to sea and across the town, and the occasional glimpse into sequestered cloisters. Entrances to the wall walk are marked (A) on the illustration on the following page.

MAJOR FORTIFICATIONS

MINČETA TOWER: This classic chess-piece tower was built to replace a smaller, squatter fort that had stood on the same site. After the fall of Constantinople in 1453, Ragusa decided to strengthen its defences, and plans for a massive landward fort were drawn up. Plague delayed the start of building, which was supervised by the great Florentine architect Michelozzo (also employed on the Rector's Palace, *see pp. 57 and 93*). When his other commitments forced Michelozzo to leave Dubrovnik, work on the Minčeta was completed (in 1464) by the local stonemason Juraj Dalmatinac. The tower, at one time used to store water, takes its name from the noble Menčetić family, who presumably funded its construction.

Michelozzo's Minčeta tower dominates Dubrovnik's landward fortifications with its sheer girth and strength.

FORT BOKAR: This is another design by Michelozzo, who is famed for his ability to combine massy strength with a pleasing elegance of line. It was completed in 1570, having taken almost 100 years to build. Cannons were fired from it in times of peace to test their range. During the 19th century, when Austria controlled Dalmatia, Fort Bokar was used as a prison. One of its inmates was Arthur Evans, the British archaeologist who later went on to fame for uncovering the ruins of Knossos on Crete. In 1882 he was working for the *Manchester Guardian*, writing on

THE FORTS, GATES & BASTIONS

ACCESS TO THE WALLS:
A On Sv. Dominika, next to St Luke's chapel;

B Just inside the Pile gate;
C On Od Pustijerne: follow signs to the Maritime Museum.

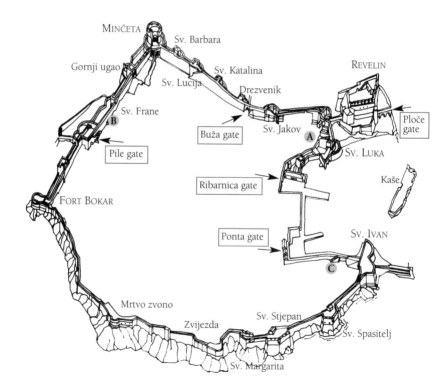

Fort Lovrijenac rises impregnably above the tiny harbour of Brsalje, protecting approaches to the city from the south-west.

Balkan affairs, and making forays into Herzegovina that led the Austrian government to arrest him on charges of espionage. He was released after six weeks, but banished from Austria and her dominions.

PILE GATE: The outer gate with its Renaissance archway dates from 1537. It boasts the city's oldest effigy of St Blaise. The drawbridge is by the municipal engineer Miličević. The Gothic inner gate is almost a century earlier. This time the effigy of St Blaise is the city's most recent, the work of the sculptor Ivan Meštrović (*see p. 99*).

PLOČE GATE & REVELIN: The Ploče gate is similar in design to the Pile gate, with outer and inner gates and a drawbridge. The Revelin fortress, whose main function was to protect the city against landward Turkish attack, is incorporated into the outer gate. When it was being built, all Ragusan citizens resident outside the old town had to contribute a stone.

FORT ST JOHN (SV. IVAN): Today's fort dates from 1557, a joining together of two earlier fortresses according to plans by Miličević. It is now home to the Maritime Museum (*see p. 100*).

FORT LOVRIJENAC: This massive free-standing fortress above the suburb of Pile was designed to repel sea attack. During the Italian occupation in the Second World War it was used as a prison. Today it is one of the favourite venues for open-air theatre during the Summer Festival (see *p. 186*). It is open to the public in summer as well. A ticket to the city walls gains you access.

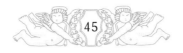

MAJOR SIGHTS
OF THE OLD TOWN

The major sights covered in this book are listed below. Numbers refer to the map on the following page.

❶ THE OLD PORT - p. 48

❺ THE FRANCISCAN FRIARY - p. 68

❷ THE STRADUN - p. 51

❻ THE DOMINICAN FRIARY - p. 72

❸ THE RECTOR'S PALACE - p. 57

❼ THE CHURCH OF ST BLAISE - p. 76

❹ THE SPONZA PALACE - p. 66

❽ THE CATHEDRAL - p. 78

Map of Dubrovnik showing the old town, old port and major fortifications, with Pile, Gruž and Rijeka Dubrovačka on the far left.

RAGVSA

MAJOR SIGHTS OF THE OLD TOWN

1 OLD PORT
2 STRADUN
3 RECTOR'S PALACE
4 SPONZA PALACE

5 FRANCISCAN FRIARY
6 DOMINICAN FRIARY
7 CHURCH OF ST BLAISE
8 CATHEDRAL

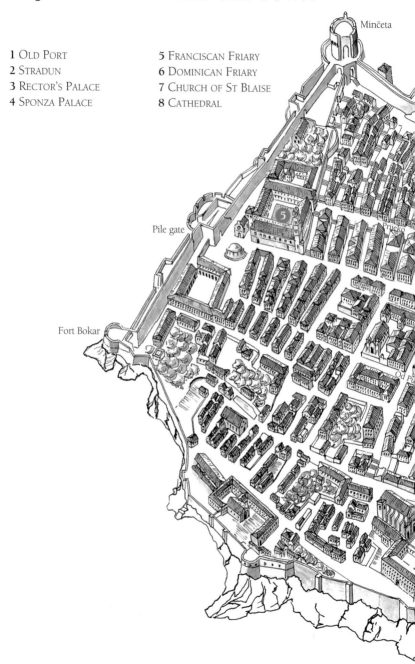

Minčeta

Pile gate

Fort Bokar

Prijeko

Od P

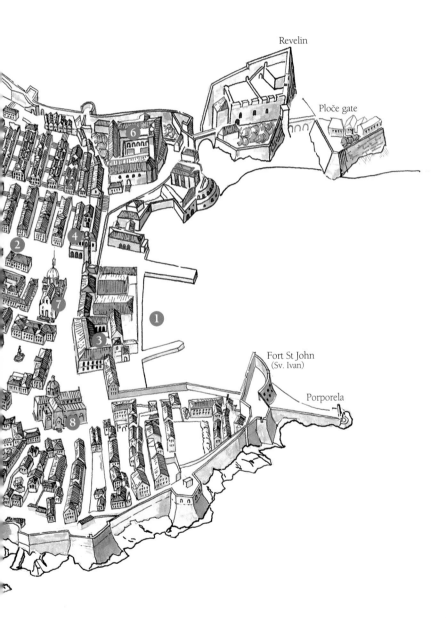

Revelin

Ploče gate

Fort St John
(Sv. Ivan)

Porporela

THE OLD PORT
(Stara Luka)

The old port of Dubrovnik presents a peaceful and picturesque scene today. Once the hub of Ragusa's commercial and maritime activity, the fulcrum upon which her existence turned and crucible of her prosperity, it has now relinquished that role to the harbour of Gruž, and most of the ships that dock in the old port today are pleasure cruisers or the old rigged and masted fishing vessels that seldom use their sails, nor do they go out to fish, but instead motor visitors off for fish picnics at Cavtat and the Elaphite Islands (*see pp. 155 & 170*).

Built close within the embrace of the old city walls, the port and its two docks are protected from the south-east by the fortress of St John (Sv. Ivan) and the breakwater known as Porporela, from which one can enjoy a view of the island of Lokrum, a favourite place for day trips, and famed for its deadly curse (*see p. 150*). The northern side is protected by the fortress of St Luke (Sv. Luka). An open-air fishmarket used to be held in the wide paved square that opens

View of the old port from outside the Ploče gate. The rounded arches of the former arsenal are clearly visible between the two docks.

out from the larger of the two docks. Today that space is filled with barrows and stalls selling souvenirs. Local fishermen do still put out to sea at night in their tiny skiffs, though. Sometimes you can hear them singing as they mend their nets. More often you can glimpse them playing cards and drinking beer in the Miho Pracat mariners' club in the alley named Kneza Damjana Jude, linked to the smaller dock by a gateway in the wall. Today any fisherman with a catch sets up a stand at this end of the port. Cats wait patiently for scraps while the old-town housewives inspect the merchandise.

The most important feature of the old port was its arsenal, a miniature version of Venice's Arsenale. We know that the arsenal existed by 1272, although the likelihood is that it is several centuries older even than that. In the late 15th century it was improved and extended by the Republic's official engineer Pasko Miličević (*see p. 93*), who was also the architect of the Kaše harbour wall, and responsible for planning a number of the city's defences, especially the manner in which the various fortresses are linked. Many of his plans were not carried out until the second half of the 16th century, however, at a time when Venice was harrying the Republic.

The Kaše mole, which bulks out of the harbour midway along a diagonal axis between the suburb of Ploče and Fort St John, was used as a wave-break and also as a method of defence: just as a great chain protected the mouth of the Golden Horn at Constantinople, so heavy chains were stretched from Kaše across either side of the Ragusa harbour entrance to prevent hostile ships from entering the port. Popular legend tells of a certain Ambrosini, head of the Ragusan artillery, who ran out of cannon wadding when firing on hostile Venetian craft. Undaunted by the crisis, he whipped off his wig and ordered that that be stuffed inside the cannon instead.

The three archways of the arsenal that you see today are all that remain of a larger complex demolished in 1863, at a time when maritime threat had receded, and the prosperous middle classes were thinking more of pleasure than of serious seafaring: a theatre was erected instead, and its first performance was a Verdi opera.

The old Ragusan argosies would sail right inside the archways to be housed in times of bad weather, as well as to be loaded and unloaded or to receive essential repairs. Because of its wide arches, the shipyard formed a weak point in the city's defences, so the arches were bricked up when not in use. Every time an argosy sailed in or out the bricks were removed and replaced. Today the

Cleaning fishing nets in the old port after a day's catch.

arsenal plays host to the city's best known café and a popular meeting point, the Gradska Kavana. Once a very grand place where smart dress (and a tie for men) was *de rigueur*, it is much more free and easy now. It boasts two outdoor terraces: one to the west overlooking the Church of St Blaise (Sv. Vlaho, *see p. 76*) and Luža Square, and the other to the east, overlooking the port. On the other side of the large dock, in the old harbourmaster's office, is the Pizzeria Poklisar (the *poklisari* were the Ragusan Republic's emissaries to Bosnia and Turkey), which will serve you a quick snack as you wait for your boat to come in.

THE STRADUN

'Stradun has seen almost all the monarchs of the world, state presidents, drunkards and bums, famous musicians and actors, prominent authors, philosophers and painters. These have all walked from the narrow Pile Gate to Ploče, each of them leaving a trace of their spirit and their thoughts.' So says Tomislav Durbešić in *Upon Visiting Dubrovnik*, written in 1991. It is certainly a bold claim, and perhaps laced with a certain amount of wishful thinking. For there is nothing really grand about the Stradun. That is its great charm. Before the earthquake of 1667 it was lined by exuberant Renaissance palaces. Now only one of these remains: the Sponza Palace (*see p. 66*) at the east end. After the earthquake the Stradun was re-landscaped by a Roman engineer, Giulio Cerruti. All the buildings are of uniform height, with uniformly green-painted window frames and shutters, and a uniform configuration of arched doorway and display window at street level, purpose-built to accommodate shops. The system of trundling wares to these shops on hand-carts is much the same now as it was when the shops first went into business. Though these late 17th-century houses

The Stradun on a rainy day in spring, its paved surface glassy as a mirror.

are not architectural *tours de force*, they create a feeling of harmonious restraint which is extremely pleasing.

The official name of this great 292-metre, heterogeneous arterial promenade is Placa. Its vernacular name, Stradun, was allegedly coined by a Milanese officer in the Austro-Hungarian army, who upon glimpsing it through the city gates for the first time exclaimed '*Che stradone!*: What a vast street!'

Once upon a time it was not a street at all, but a shallow, marshy channel that divided the Romanised island of Ragusium from the Slav-inhabited mainland under the craggy limestone shadow of Mt Srđ. Over the years this channel began to silt up, and eventually, in the 12th century, the citizens filled it in entirely, in order to merge their city with its Slavic suburbs. Originally the Stradun was paved with red brick; it was first flagged with stone in the mid 15th century, and the actual paving that covers it now dates from 1901. Today those century-old stones are so highly polished by passing feet that the effect looks very much like the water it once was.

The Stradun runs west to east, with the Pile gate at the west end. At the east end stands the city belltower and archway leading onto the waterfront and port, and

The large Onofrian fountain (1438), terminus of Dubrovnik's first piped water supply.

the steeply walled alleyway leading out to the Ploče gate, an alley which in summertime fills with swifts, darting and diving between their nests and the sky. Just inside the inner Pile Gate, to the left, lies the votive church of the Holy Saviour (Sv. Spas, *see p. 103*). To the right stands the **Large Onofrian Fountain**, where teenagers congregate, and which was built in 1438 by the Neapolitan hydro-engineer Onofrio della Cava, who created the city's first mains water supply by pumping water twelve kilometres from Rijeka Dubrovačka, to gush from this fountain into the grateful citizens' pitchers. Not that the citizens were grateful to begin with. In fact they

The Small Onofrian Fountain, with the Sponza Palace in the background.

were highly sceptical that the plan would work, and threatened to have della Cava arraigned as an impostor. Fortunately for everyone, della Cava knew exactly what he was doing, and his water system functioned impeccably. The fountain itself is an austere-looking creation (it has suffered severe damage twice: in the earthquake of 1667 and the siege of 1991–92), a team effort by della Cava and the Milanese architect Pietro di Martino. Right at the opposite end of the Stradun is the **Small Onofrian Fountain**, where the pigeons bathe. This was built in the same year and by the same team: della Cava the engineer responsible for making sure it functioned properly, and di Martino the architect responsible for making sure it pleased the eye.

One of the Stradun's other well-known landmarks is the **Orlando column**, just outside the church of St Blaise. This docile-looking, doe-eyed individual is supposed to represent none other than Ariosto's Orlando Furioso, Count of Brittany and Paladin of Charlemagne, eight feet tall, a flower of chivalry, and the much-sung hero of the *Chanson de Roland*. According to legend Roland (Orlando) led a campaign to defend Ragusa against Saracen marauders in the 9th century—

a legend which, sad to say, is untrue, since Roland famously fell at Roncesvalles in August 778, victim of a Basque ambush. Over the years, however, those Basques were transformed by minstrel tradition into Saracens, and it is an attested fact that monuments to Roland were commonly erected in free towns across the Holy Roman Empire, the most famous surviving example being in Bremen. This Ragusan version was not erected by Charlemagne, however, but by Bonino da Milano, in 1418, harking back to the Carolingian use of Roland's image as the symbol of a free merchant state. In his hand the Ragusan Orlando holds his famous indestructible sword, Durandal, which at the moment of his untimely death he flung into a poisoned river to prevent it falling to the enemy. Its hilt was alleged to contain a thread from the Virgin's cloak, one of St Peter's teeth, a hair from the head of St Denis, and a drop of St Basil's blood. During the heyday of the Republic new laws were proclaimed from the statue steps: boring but important municipal matters from the lowest step, more momentous announcements from the middle one, and life-and-death decisions involving war from the topmost. Petty felons were chained here to do public penance, and condemned men exhibited as a deterrent example. When Napoleon's hegemony began to falter and his Illyrian Provinces began to dissolve, Dubrovnik optimistically re-declared her

The Orlando Column.

independence, and hoisted her Libertas banner from Orlando's flagstaff. The Congress of Vienna affirmed Austria's right to control Dalmatia, however, and the flag was solemnly and sheepishly lowered again. Today the Libertas flag is flown here once again, but for a different reason: to proclaim the beginning of the Dubrovnik Summer Festival.

On the statue's plinth, below Orlando's feet, you can see the faint etching of a straight line. This—originally, they say, the length of the great Saracen-buster's forearm—was used as the yardstick for the Ragusan cubit or standard unit of length (the *lakat*), which measured 51.2 centimetres.

During the siege of 1991–92 the Stradun suffered 45 direct hits by mortar shells. Though the roofs and façades have been repaired now, the scattered starburst pockmarks in the glassy surface of the pavement survive to tell the tale. At one point the street was so deserted that grass grew up between the flagstones—something unheard-of in the history of a city which is not exactly famous for its flora and fauna. Today, however, it is business as usual on the Stradun, with open-air cafés doing a roaring trade, local lovelies and likelies sauntering up and down, and the cheeky, ever-optimistic restaurant touts out-pattering each other to nab your custom. If you're trying to make contact with someone, the best thing to do is to sit in the Stradun and wait for them to pass by. Sooner or later they will. As one local resident put it, communication on the Stradun is 'easier than on the Internet'.

THE RECTOR'S PALACE

(Knežev Dvor) Open Mon–Sat 9am–2pm (winter) and 9am–6pm (summer)

The Rector's Palace in its original form would have looked more like a bulky fortress than a grand and elegant mansion. In the early 15th century, however, this fortress was blown to smithereens by an explosion in the arsenal's nearby gunpowder magazine. The Senate immediately decided to erect a 'more magnificent construction, sparing no expense', and the man they hired to do the job was Onofrio della Cava (*see Stradun section above*). Della Cava's palace was built in Venetian Gothic style, and by all accounts was very magnificent. But once again, disaster struck. Not having learned their lesson about the volatility of gunpowder magazines, the Ragusans continued to store their ammunition a mere stone's throw from the seat of their government—and sure enough, only thirty years after the first explosion, the magazine blew up again, and della Cava's palace went up in smoke with it. The man hired by the senate to produce

The loggia of the Rector's Palace. The building is an interesting fusion of Venetian Gothic and Renaissance elements, the Renaissance flavour having been introduced by the great Florentine architect Michelozzo Michelozzi.

a new building was the Forentine Michelozzo, who was working on strengthening the city walls at the time. Michelozzo sought to introduce Ragusa to the Renaissance, the style which had originated—largely under his direction—in Florence about forty years previously. In this case, however, he was pressed for time (he was working simultaneously on Cosimo de' Medici's new palace in Florence), and instead of demolishing della Cava's ruins and starting from scratch, he grafted his own work onto what remained from before. The result, completed in 1464, is an interesting intermarriage, creating a building which has been described as 'a small masterpiece' and 'one of the most beautiful buildings in Dalmatia'.

The upper floor clearly incorporates della Cava's work in the Venetian Gothic windows. The ground floor has a beautiful arcade of round Renaissance arches supported by columns of Korčula stone, which proved strong enough to withstand the 1667 earthquake. The capitals that top these columns seem to include work by both men. The three central capitals are more classical in style and thought to be by Michelozzo. The four outer capitals, generally considered to be more interesting, are attributed to della Cava—the carving itself is more probably the work of Pietro di Martino, della Cava's collaborator on the Onofrian fountains. The outermost capital to the right represents Aesculapius in his laboratory. Aesculapius, the Graeco-Roman god of medicine,

Aesculapius in his laboratory, one of the capitals from the Rector's Palace.

son of Apollo, is said to have been born at Epidaurus, which in local minds was easily conflated with their own Epidaurum, present-day Cavtat (*see p. 170*). Depicting the god on a pillar was a conspicuous attempt to demonstrate a seamless link between modern Ragusa and the glorious classical past.

The main entranceway is thought to be Michelozzo's design, and the carved reliefs of Venus and Cupid seducing Mars (the mastery of love over strife), of

The tympanum above the 'Gate of Charity',
showing Charity feeding her hungry brood.

naked youths disporting themselves among vines, of winged putti playing the organ, of a bear fighting a dragon—to mention only a few—are attributed to the local stonemason Paulus Ragusinus. The main door was only opened on state occasions, when the robed Rector and Council members would issue forth and place themselves on the stone seats that line the porch, where tourists in their shorts and T-shirts now loll indolently, and where an elderly local lady feeds her black dog Bobby every morning. Not that the Council grandees were above a bit of indolence themselves. Sometimes they came out into the porch to watch open-air performances of the work of local dramatists, for example that of Marin Držić (*see p. 132*)—though he would not have felt particularly honoured, as he spent a lot of his spare time criticising the ruling elite.

The small doorway to the right of the main entrance is known as the Gate of Charity—hence the painted tympanum depicting a voluptuous woman with naked, munificent breasts, surrounded by a hungry brood of infants. In times of famine—which struck three times in the first half of the 16th century—the poor and indigent of the town would line up outside this door to receive free handouts of grain.

INSIDE THE RECTOR'S PALACE

The main atrium again contains a mélange of Gothic and Renaissance. It is famous for its excellent acoustics, which is why it is a popular concert venue during the Summer Festival (*see p. 186*). The bust in the centre is of prosperous Ragusan merchant Miho Pracat (*see p. 157*). Pracat died childless, and left his enormous

Bust of the mariner Miho Pracat, in the atrium of the Rector's Palace. Pracat died without heirs, and left all his fortune to the Ragusan Republic.

fortune to the Republic. Ragusa returned the gesture by putting up this memorial to him—Pracat is the only commoner to be so honoured. To the left of the main entrance are the old administrative offices. The notary's office has been recreated, with painted wooden panelling and a long meeting table. Citizens would come here to make their wills, bring actions against their neighbours, draw up deeds of sale and purchase, etc.

THE DUNGEONS

Underneath the lower, right-hand loggia were the state prisons, where some of the offenders were walled up alive, and where the most heinous crimes were punished with the worst cells—the ones that flooded at high tide. The right-hand of the two doors leads to these. On the lintel is etched a lion's face. Through the left-hand door are displays of wooden trunks with complicated lock mechanisms, and architectural fragments, including vestiges of wall painting: the words 'Ave Maria' and a niche that held a votive statue, from a part of the building that once belonged to the harbour complex. The furthest room, the vaulted, stucco-ceilinged former courtroom, contains portraits of Ragusan notables, including Nikolica Bunić, Marojica Kaboga, Marin Getaldić and Ivan Gundulić.

DEATH IN THE LINE OF DUTY: THE STORY OF BUNIĆ & KABOGA

Both men were from patrician Ragusan families, and both served their republic as emissaries to Turkey and Bosnia. **Marojica Kaboga** began badly, by murdering his father-in-law outside the Rector's Palace and being clapped in irons as a result. The chaos of the 1667 earthquake allowed him to escape, however, after which he appears to have been forgiven. He was sent as emissary (*poklisar*) to Constantinople, where the notoriously tribute-hungry Grand Vizier, Kara Mustafa, was demanding compensation on behalf of aggrieved Bosnian merchants, who complained that Ragusa levied unfair

Nikolica Bunić.

taxes on their goods. When Ragusa refused to pay any compensation, Kaboga was flung into gaol and the Ban of Bosnia was ordered to cease trading with the Republic. **Nikolica Bunić** was sent to Bosnia to negotiate a settlement; the Ban remained obdurate and determined to carry out Kara Mustafa's wishes. He incarcerated Bunić in a noisome dungeon. Before they set out on their missions, Ragusan emissaries were sternly warned that 'the Republic is watching you', and Bunić knew that his instructions were not to yield. He caught plague in prison and died. Kaboga survived. When the Turkish armies were defeated by Russia in 1678, the Sublime Porte became more willing to come to terms, and settled for a reduced payment, with a personal payment to Kara Mustafa thrown in as well. Alas for the greedy Grand Vizier. Only a few years later, in 1683, he was defeated before the gates of Vienna, and never saw Turkish soil again.

THE FORMER COURTROOMS

At the top of the atrium's right-hand stairway there are two carved capitals. The one on the right shows a female figure representing Justice. The companion capital on the left shows the Rector administering the same. Some commentators have remarked that the carvings in the Rector's Palace are rather crude. This may be because Michelozzo, in a rush to get to his next commission on time, left the bulk of the work to local stonemasons—although that is an ungracious accusation to make, because we know that the man he left in charge was the highly skilled Juraj Dalmatinac (also known as Giorgio Orsini). The most likely fault lies with the building material itself. Korčula stone, while ideal for withstanding anything the Richter scale can throw at it, is notoriously difficult to carve.

The stairway leads to the Republic's former arsenal and judicial chambers. These now contain an exhibition of Ragusan coins, weaponry and pharmacist's paraphernalia, as well as some portraits of famous citizens, for example the mathematician Ruđer Bošković (*see p. 84*), and the Renaissance beauty and poetess, the almond-eyed, rosebud-lipped Cvijeta Zuzorić, to whom an admiring Tasso dedicated a number of sonnets.

THE STATE APARTMENTS

The atrium's left-hand stairway leads to the upper loggia and the entrance to the former state apartments. Fire, Frenchmen and Austrians are the three furies commonly blamed for the sorry state of those apartments today. Fire also destroyed the next-door Great Council chambers. The doorway that linked the two buildings still survives, but the building, gutted in 1816, does not.

For the duration of his one month's mandate the Rector was forbidden to bring his family to live with him in the palace . Nor was he allowed to set foot outside the palace doors during the whole period. To make the position bearable, we must assume that the interior was fairly splendid. We know that it was this wing of the palace that was used for state functions and receptions of foreign dignitaries, and that it was here that the Rector had his living quarters. Most of what you see in the state apartments today, however, is a reconstruction. The current furnishings throw back only a pale reflection of what would once have been. The main rooms on public view are described below.

THE STATE APARTMENTS

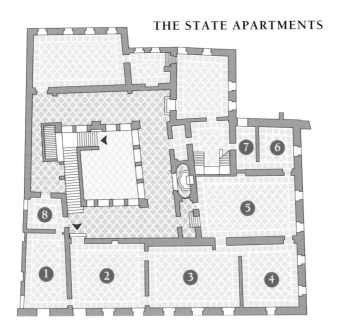

1 THE ANTECHAMBER
2 THE ROCOCO SALON
3 THE LOUIS SEIZE SALON
4 THE RECTOR'S STUDY

5 THE MUSIC ROOM
6 THE SLEEPING CABINET
7 THE 18TH-CENTURY ROOM
8 THE ENTRANCE LOBBY

1 THE ANTECHAMBER: A long, narrow apartment containing 18th-century furniture and portraits of Ragusan patricians.

2 THE ROCOCO SALON: A large, light front-facing room containing more 18th-century furniture, and more portraits of Ragusan patricians.

3 THE LOUIS SEIZE SALON: A com-panion salon to the Rococo, containing furniture in the Neoclassical style and a collection of derivative art (School of Bassano, School of Guido Reni, a copy of Rubens). The best painting is an anonymous 17th-century Dutch study of a grandfather and grandson.

4 THE RECTOR'S STUDY: Hung in red silk, with a recreation of the Rector's writing desk, with a dummy Rector in crimson robes behind it. A marquetry box contains copies of the keys to the city gates, which were in the Rector's keeping. The study also contains a highly distinctive *Baptism of Christ* (1509) by the Ragusan master Mihajlo Hamzić, which was commissioned for the Rector's Palace in 1508, and by some miracle survives. The scene shows an angel with Fra Angelico-style rainbow wings holding a bathing sheet in readiness as Christ stands up to his knees in the swirling Jordan, with John the Baptist about to tip water on him from a golden jug. A kingfisher sits and watches from the bank.

On the opposite wall is *Venus and Adonis* by Paris Bordone.

5 THE MUSIC ROOM: An early 19th-century Viennese spinet (currently being restored) gives this room its name. The large clock on an inlaid chest of drawers between the windows was a gift from Auguste Frédéric Marmont, Napoleon's marshal, who was created Duke of Ragusa in 1808. The clock face is

Recreation of the Rector's study inside the Rector's Palace. Above the desk to the right hangs Mihajlo Hamzić's Baptism of Christ *(see p. 95).*

inscribed, '*Marmont duc de Raguse en reconnaisance* [sic] *au maire de Raguse 1809*'.

6 THE SLEEPING CABINET: A re-creation of the Rector's bedroom, with 18th-century furnishings.

7 THE 18TH-CENTURY ROOM: This small lobby, with stairs (roped off) to the upper floor, has two classical *vedute* and 18th-century furniture.

8 THE ENTRANCE LOBBY: This was once the antechamber between the Rector's apartments and the next-door Great Council chambers. Those were gutted by fire in 1816. The present building on the site (the Dubrovnik Town Hall), dates from the mid 19th century. The original doorway that linked the two buildings still survives, carved with the Periclean motto '*Obliti privatorum, publica curate*' (Forget private concerns, think of the public good). Just inside the doorway are three 18th-century sedan chairs, the preferred mode of transport for Ragusa's noble ladies. Ragusan women were noted for their piety and modesty, and society seems to have been sufficiently influenced by Ottoman custom for women barely to have shown themselves in public at all. It was not until the Jesuits came to the city that women were persuaded even to leave their houses for Sunday Mass. Before that a Ragusan gentlewoman would worship in her family's private chapel.

THE SPONZA PALACE

This beautiful little building, Ragusa's former customs house and state mint, is the best example of Venetian-influenced architecture remaining in Dubrovnik. The hooded windows with their curlicue tracery on the first floor are pure Venetian Gothic, while the top floor is late Renaissance. The upper part of the building was designed in the early 16th century by Pasko Miličević (*see p. 93*)—his last great project and his masterpiece—and the building work was carried out by stonemasons from Korčula, the Andrijić brothers, who were also involved in repairing damage done to the Rector's Palace by an earth tremor in 1520. The Renaissance portico on the ground floor, which conceals the plain and more sombre older part of the building, was probably added in the 16th century too.

Fortunately for posterity, the damage that the Sponza sustained in the severe 1667 earthquake was not beyond repair, and because of the crucial role the Sponza played in generating the Republic's revenue, it was one of the first buildings to be restored. The Sponza gets its name from the Latin word *spongia* (sponge): a building that stood here in the 14th century had a rainwater cistern where water

The Sponza Palace, the only building on the Stradun to survive the 1667 earthquake.

from the roof was filtered by a sponge-like filter. It is also known as the Divona, a word that derives from *dogana*, the Italian for customs house. Before setting off on the arduous trip into the Balkan interior, Ragusa's merchant caravans would line up and check their loads outside the Sponza. Any merchants arriving in the town made the Sponza their first port of call (after serving their statutory term in quarantine). All their goods were examined and the amount of duty payable was calculated. Cheating was vehemently discouraged. Carved above the central archway at the far end of the oblong inner courtyard is the admonitory motto 'When I weigh merchandise with these scales, God is

Main door of the Sponza Palace.

also weighing me'. The customs house occupied the ground floor of the Sponza, and a pair of public scales used to hang in this central archway. Today the original mechanism from the city clock is on display there. The rooms leading off the courtyard, all with the names of saints carved above their doorways, were used as store-rooms. The first floor of the building was used for learned gatherings, where the Republic's scientists could expound their latest theories and literati could declaim their poetry. Hopefully their soirées were not disturbed by too much thudding and pounding from the State Mint on the floor above, busily hammering out coins of gold, silver and copper. This mint, presided over by the Rector, and run by a small board of directors chosen from among the Senate, had been going since 1337, and continued to function until the fall of the Republic. Ragusan currency—perperae, grossi and ducats—was accepted round the world, and was convertible on all foreign exchanges. The Sponza continued its life as a customs house until the beginning of the 20th century. After the Second World War it was transformed into the Museum of the Socialist Revolution. Today it houses the city's Historical Archives, and is used as an events venue during the Summer Festival.

THE FRANCISCAN FRIARY

There is a legend that Dubrovnik's first Franciscan friary was founded soon after St Francis of Assisi himself visited the town on his way to the Holy Land to evangelise the Saracens. Whatever the truth, the Franciscans (the *Mala Braća* or Minorites) are thought to have first arrived in Dubrovnik sometime in the early 13th century, to provide a bulwark of mainstream Catholicism against the heresies that were taking root in the Balkan hinterland and threatening to spread Ragusawards. To begin with mendicant friars were forbidden to reside within the city walls, and the Franciscans had a house outside the Pile gate, where the Hotel Hilton Imperial stands now. When they received a grant of land inside the walls, in the 14th century, they were set at one end of the Stradun with the Dominicans at the other, and both orders were given the task of guarding the city gates against intruders.

THE FRANCISCAN CHURCH

Little remains today of the original mediaeval church, which we know was built in a transitional style between Romanesque and Gothic. Renovations and refurbishments over the years have rendered it mainly Baroque in style now, except for its early 15th-century campanile (the copper dome is more recent) and the Pietà above the south door, the work of two local stonemasons, the Petrović brothers. The worst misfortune to befall the church was the earthquake of 1667. Although the Pietà miraculously survived, the church interior was gutted by fire, and all its treasures—sumptuous gold plate and paintings by Italian Renaissance masters—were lost.

THE CHURCH INTERIOR

The spirit of the interior is entirely Baroque: a large, rectangular hall articulated by decorative adjuncts, in this case elaborate altarpieces, stucco-work, and an organ loft carved with musical putti. The main altar surround, with its four gleaming Solomonic columns, is the work of Celio of Ancona (1712), while its statue of the *Risen Christ* is thought to be the work of Marino Gropelli, architect of St Blaise's church. On the north wall is the altar of the Sacred Heart, offering hope to the hopeless, with a carved and gilded statue of Madonna and Child,

Gothic Pietà *above the main entrance to the Franciscan church.*

crowned with the diadems of heaven, washing away original sin and triumphing over the apple and the serpent, which writhes corkscrew-like at their feet. Also on the north wall is the altar of St Francis, who is shown praying in the wilderness, with rabbits and foxes cohabiting in harmony behind him. On the ground just in front of this altar is a flagstone marking the tomb of Anica Bošković, sister of Ruđer (*see p. 84*). Anica, who died at the age of 90, was a deeply devout woman, known for her poetical satires on 18th-century decadence in Ragusan society.

Opposite St Francis, on the south wall, is an altarpiece showing the Virgin with an upturned crescent moon and a dragon in its death throes at her feet, as described in the Book of Revelation: '*And there appeared a great wonder in heaven; a woman clothed with the sun, and the moon under her feet: and the dragon stood before the woman. And she brought forth a man child, who was to rule all nations with a rod of iron. And the great dragon was cast out*'.

On the pulpit, note the wooden arm, robed in Franciscan brown, which holds the crucifix aloft. To the left of the high altar steps is a marble slab commemorating Gjivo Gundulić (Ivan Gundulić, *see p. 132*), Ragusa's great epic poet and father of modern Croatian, who is buried here.

THE FRANCISCAN CLOISTER

The Franciscan friary contains the most peaceful and beautiful courtyard in the city: its cloister, a miniature oasis of tranquillity; cool and green in the summer months, with palm trees and clipped box hedges interspersed with flashes of purple bougainvillea and oleander, rose bushes and a grapefruit tree. It is the work of Mihoje Brajkov (Micha di Antivari), from Bar in Montenegro, who died in Dubrovnik, of plague, in 1348. He is commemorated as 'magister Micha, who made this cloister' by a tablet in the cloister, halfway up the pillar in the south-east corner (straight ahead at the end as you enter).

Each side of the cloister's colonnade is divided into three hexaphorae (six-light bays) by pairs of slender, eight-sided columns, their capitals decorated by fanciful Romanesque-style demons, humorous grotesques, human faces, birds and animals. One of the capitals—the second straight ahead of you as you go in—shows a head with a very swollen cheek. This is said to be Brajkov's own caricature of himself, as he was suffering from raging toothache at the time. In the centre of the cloister is a raised walk with a stone bench on either side. (Note

Bougainvillea and agapanthus in the Franciscan cloister.

Capital with a swollen cheek, allegedly the sculptor's own self-parody.

the cows' heads with their long tongues on the capital as you enter.) A small fountain here is topped by a statue of St Francis displaying his stigmata. Behind him is a particularly appealing capital with dogs.

The friary is also noted for its ancient dispensary. Founded in 1317, it is the oldest continuously functioning pharmacy in Europe. Originally it was used exclusively by the friars, but as the city grew, the pressures of urban living made some sort of public health facility essential, and donations were made with the aim of turning the pharmacy into a public institution. Its pestles and mortars and its alembics were used to concoct anything and everything from remedies for itching fleabites to secret philtres for—well, who knows; they were secret. Medicine at the time was a horrifying mixture of misapplied science and hocus-pocus, but some of the friars' herbal recipes probably brought relief. If you dare, you can even put them to the test. The pharmacy at the entrance to the cloister still functions, and sells little pots of creams and lotions dated 1317, and apparently made to original recipes. *Open Mon–Sat 8am–2pm.*

THE FRIARY MUSEUM

The two best exhibits are a small painting of St Blaise on wood by Lovro Dobričević (*see p. 96*), and a copy of a painting showing Dubrovnik before the 1667 earthquake. A Sunday-morning procession winds its way from the Church of All Saints into od Puča. It is interesting to see how Venetian the Rector's Palace looked, how ornate the large Onofrian fountain was, and how many arcaded palaces lined the Stradun. Other things of note are the 18th-century pharmacy furnishings, and a little oil sketch of a girl admiring another's engagement ring (in fact a double portrait of his wife) by Vlaho Bukovac (*see p. 98*)—an entirely secular scene; it is rather surprising to find it here. There is also an exquisite *Ecce Homo* by Francesco Francia, showing Christ in a room, with all the sorrow of the world in his weeping eyes, and a glimpse of the landscape of Paradise through a corner of window behind.

THE DOMINICAN FRIARY

The Dominicans first came to Ragusa from Italy soon after their order was founded in the early 13th century. Together with the Franciscans at Pile and the Benedictines on Lokrum, the Dominicans' aim was to help stamp out the rumblings of heresy that were seeping coastwards from the interior. They established their present friary, which nestles under the protective aegis of the Ploče bastions, in the early 14th century. From 1390 right up until the mid-20th century it remained a seat of philosophical and theological study.

Balustrade walled up at the bottom so that women's ankles would not be seen and distract the friars from their orations. Knees are now visible instead.

The friary and its church are reached by climbing a Gothic balustraded stairway from ulica Sv. Dominika. The lower part of the balustrade was intentionally walled up so that women's ankles wouldn't be seen (*see picture*). On your right at the top you will see the former chapel of St Sebastian, now an art gallery ❶. Opposite is a church built for the merchants' guild the Confraternity of the Rosary ❷, which the Dominicans founded in the 13th century. It is now the seat of the Brothers of the Order of the Croatian Dragon.

THE DOMINICAN CLOISTER

The finest part of the priory is its cloister ❸, where orange and lemon trees give colour in winter, and whose cool calm is especially welcome on a hot day. This cloister is Dubrovnik's earliest example of sacred Renaissance architecture. It was built between 1456 and 1483, mainly following plans by Maso di Bartolommeo from Florence, though the local architects who were employed to carry out the work couldn't help giving the round Renaissance arches a more

Gothic feel. Twenty triphorae (three-light bays), five on each side, enclose a square patio with a well at its centre. During the Napoleonic occupation, the Dominican complex was requisitioned to house the French cavalry. Shallow eating troughs for the horses were gouged out of the stone between the pillars in the cloister—and are still there today—and the church itself was used as a stable. The cloister was restored in 1900 with funds donated by Ignatius Amerling, a public-spirited citizen whose family was full of schemes for municipal improvement. Thanks to him, the memory of all those whinnying war-horses has been all but extinguished.

1 FORMER CHAPEL OF ST SEBASTIAN
  (NOW THE GALERIJA SEBASTIAN)
2 CHURCH OF THE ROSARY
3 CLOISTER

4 DOMINICAN FRIARY CHURCH
5 FRIARY MUSEUM, MAIN WING
6 SACRISTY

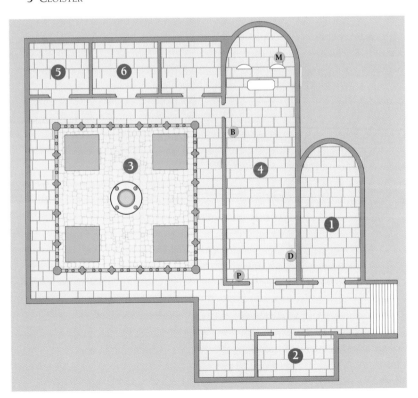

THE DOMINICAN CHURCH

The church nowadays ④ is a cavernous, echoing rectangle, redeemed from austerity by its beautiful five-sided Gothic apse, lit by two boldly colourful stained glass lancets. Most of the fine works of art that used to hang in the church have been removed to the friary museum (*see below*). In some ways this is a shame, although works by modern Croatian masters have succeeded them, and one important treasure has survived *in situ*: the large gilt and painted crucifix that hangs inside the central arch at the head of the nave. Acquired and installed in 1358, it is the work of Paolo Veneziano. The church also contains examples of the work of four major modern Croatian artists, three of them Ragusan. There is a mosaic altarpiece by Ivo Dulčić

Interior of the Dominican church.

(1916–1975) ⓓ, an oil painting of the Holy Family ⓟ by Đuro Pulitika (b. 1922), a statue of the Virgin and child and a bas-relief of the Descent from the Cross by Ivan Meštrović (1883–1962) ⓜ, and a painting by Vlaho Bukovac (1855–1922) ⓑ, a sentimentally dramatic scene of St Dominic curing a liverish child.

THE DOMINICAN FRIARY MUSEUM

The main wing of the museum ⑤ houses works from the Dubrovnik School of the 15th and 16th centuries. First and foremost among these are three paintings by Nikola Božidarević (Nicola Ragusano, d. 1517). Straight ahead as you enter is *Our Lady with Saints* (1514), an altarpiece commissioned by the Đorđić family. The tiny bearded figure kneeling in the right-hand corner is the donor. To the right of this hangs *The Annunciation* (1513), commissioned by Marko Kolendić, a ship's captain from Lopud. His galleon is shown at anchor in the bay of Lopud in the central panel of the predella, below the main image. Božidarević's masterpiece is the third work, a triptych (1501) showing the Virgin and Child flanked by St Blaise and St Paul on the left, and Thomas Aquinas with a model of the Dominican church and St Augustine on the right. Two other much-prized pieces from the Dubrovnik School are a triptych by Mihajlo Hamzić (1512), showing St Nicholas in the centre, John the Baptist and St Stephen on the left, and Mary Magdalene and St Mark on the right. The other is a polyptych by Lovro Dobričević (1448). The central panel shows the *Baptism of Christ*. Above that the Virgin and Child are flanked by St Dominic and St Peter the Martyr, who was the first man to die for the Dominican cause. Originally a Cathar heretic, he was converted by St Dominic, whereupon he became a zealous preacher and inquisitor of heretics. He had an immensely popular following, despite—or perhaps because of—the salacious accusation that he habitually smuggled women into his cell. He is depicted here with a hatchet in his head and a dagger in his shoulder, as symbols of his death at the hands of two brigands who ambushed him while he was on his way from Como to Milan.

St Peter the Martyr by Lovro Dobričević.

Star exhibit in the monastery sacristy next door **6** is the painting of *Mary Magdalene with SS Raphael, Blaise and Tobias* (1554), by Titian. The kneeling figure in the foreground is a portrait of the donor, a member of the Pucić family. It has been surmised that the donor and his wife were called Raffaele and Maddalena, hence the choice of main figures in the work. There is also a 17th-century *Assumption of the Virgin*, interesting for its panorama of Dubrovnik, and a Byzantinesque altarpiece of Madonna and Child surrounded by 17th-century Mannerist saints.

THE CHURCH OF ST BLAISE
(Sv. Vlaho)

The first church on this site was erected to give thanks for the ending of the great plague outbreak in 1348. Though this original mediaeval church was not too badly damaged in the 1667 earthquake, luck did not remain on its side, and it was consumed by fire in the early 18th century. The 18th century in Dubrovnik was a time of gentle, urbanely comfortable decadence. The town was still rich enough to commission art and monuments, but not culturally robust or dynamic enough to continue to forge its own distinctly Ragusan style. The church of St Blaise, completed in 1715 by the Venetian architect Marino Gropelli, is a good example of its period—pleasing, not ground-breaking, and fitting very snugly into its surroundings. Nevertheless, as the church of the city's patron saint, it occupies a special place in all Ragusan hearts, and if there is one thing it manages to do to perfection, it is to stay true to the Dubrovnik tradition

Main façade of the Italianate church of St Blaise.

of never being too flamboyant or showy—no mean achievement when you think of some of the gilded Baroque puffballs that were going up in other parts of Europe. It is interesting to contrast the ornamentation of the main façade with the extreme austerity of the back and sides. The three statues on the roof outside represent St Blaise flanked by Faith and Hope, two virtues which declining Dubrovnik clung to rather poignantly in her sunset years. The superstitious might object to the fact that instead of having the altar facing east, the church is orientated north-to-south; but in crowded Ragusa architects had to make the best of what they were given, and the logistics of slotting buildings into the available constricted spaces often meant that conventions had to be ignored.

The interior is nicely-proportioned and compact, and rich without being gaudy. The five-piece painting on the organ loft, *The Martyrdom of St Blaise*, is by the local artist Petar Matejević (c. 1670-1726), witheringly described by one commentator as 'the only important artist' from a 'very modest period' that 'only saw the production of mediocre works'. The stained glass in the Diocletian windows is the work of one of Dubrovnik's best-known contemporary artists, Ivo Dulčić. Vividly done in bold, jolly colours, the windows look best at night, when the church is lit from within. They show (on the left) the Rector dispatching a dove, part of the traditional St Blaise's Day ceremony; (on the right) a procession with the relics of St Blaise; (above the west door) the Evangelists; (right of the sanctuary) the symbol of Dubrovnik's liberty; (left of the sanctuary) the relics of St Blaise and symbols of the Eucharist. To the right of the altar is a painting of the *Virgin and Child with St Sylvan*, whose body was brought to Dubrovnik from Rome in 1847. Depicted in bishop's robes, the saint is pointing to the city of Dubrovnik spread out behind him. The best thing in the church, however, is the gilded silver statuette of St Blaise holding a model of the pre-earthquake city, which is incorporated into the main altar. This was made by a local metalworker in the 15th century, and is the only thing to have survived intact from the original mediaeval church.

THE CATHEDRAL

According to the legend, Dubrovnik's cathedral was built with funds given by King Richard the Lionheart: during a voyage home from the Crusades he was shipwrecked on Lokrum, and vowed that if his life was spared he would build a church. What he had in mind was a tiny votive chapel on the island itself, but the Ragusans received him with such pomp and ceremony that he agreed to pay for a cathedral inside the city walls instead. There were two conditions: firstly that the Ragusans build a chapel on the

island themselves, and secondly that the Benedictine Abbot of Lokrum be permitted to celebrate mass in the cathedral on Candlemas (February 2nd) every year. This tradition became so entrenched that when the Bishop of Dubrovnik tried to abolish it in 1598, the city authorities intervened to prevent him from doing so. The Richard the Lionheart story persists even though there is no documentary evidence to support it. We know that the cathedral was built well before Richard even set out on the Crusades, and the Dubrovnik Archive states that the cathedral was built with gifts from the Ragusan nobility. If the legend does have any truth in it, it must surely be the only generous gesture that King Richard has ever been credited with.

INSIDE THE CATHEDRAL

A Byzantine basilica once stood on this site. Excavations have revealed traces of its crypt, with wall paintings showing the feet of doctors of the church and the hems of their vestments (as shown in a photograph displayed at the back of the cathedral today). Over time this church was replaced by a Romanesque cathedral. This splendid edifice, with mosaic floors, marble sedilia for the Bishop and Rector, and a graceful exterior colonnade, was destroyed in the 1667 earthquake. Stjepan Gradić, Ragusa's Ambassador to Rome and librarian at the Vatican, sat down by the banks of the Tiber and wept salt tears when he heard what had happened to his beloved city. He then asked the architect Andrea Buffalini, a native of Urbino, to design a new cathedral in the Roman Baroque style which he much admired. The Dubrovnik Senate accepted the designs, and hired the Roman architect Paolo Andreotti to execute them. The result is a beautifully simple cruciform church with a clerestory and central lantern dome, Baroque in its details and ornamentation, but overall with a much cleaner and more Classical feel. It was completed in 1713. The white colour of its interior walls, combined with the clean white stonework of its elaborate cornice, give it a lovely feeling of airiness and light, enhanced by the fact that because the cathedral has aisles, the side altars that are placed in them never dominate and crowd the atmosphere, no matter how floridly Baroque.

The most valuable painting in the cathedral hangs above the main altar. The polyptych of the *Assumption* was commissioned from Titian's studio in 1552, by

the Lazarini fraternity, as the altarpiece for their chapel of St Lazarus (on the site of the present-day Hotel Excelsior). When the cathedral was completed and lacked an altarpiece, it was decided to move the Lazarini's painting here. The left-hand panel shows St Blaise with St Lazarus, in traditional beggar's guise. The right-hand panel shows St Nicholas and St Benedict. The two smaller, upper panels depict the *Annunciation*. In the centre the Virgin is shown rising from the dead amid wondering apostles. The tomb from which she rises has the word

Venerated icon of the Virgin, in the north aisle of the cathedral.

Richly-decorated gold reliquary containing the right arm of St Blaise. This and other relics of the saint are paraded solemnly around the town on February 3rd, St Blaise's Day.

'Ticianus' written clearly upon it, leading experts to believe that this is indeed a work from the master's hand, and not merely from his studio. The cathedral's main altar itself was destroyed in the 1979 earthquake, hence the rather terrible marble thrones upholstered in grey plastic. The paintings on the chancel walls are Old Testament scenes by Padovanino. In the south transept, adjacent to the inlaid marble altar of St Bernard, is a large inscribed plaque, behind which is interred the heart of Ruđer Bošković (*see p. 84*).

The Treasury

The cathedral's main attraction is its fascinatingly macabre treasury, where the skill and imagination of Ragusa's gold and silversmiths can really be appreciated. More grisly than beautiful, the reliquaries nevertheless display some superb craftsmanship. One of the principal treasures is the reliquary containing St Blaise's head, a fine piece in enamelled gold, the work of local craftsmen, containing a part or a whole of the saint's skull. It is decorated with cartouches depicting saints, and covered with flowers made of tiny pearls fixed with gold pins, being visited by enamel bees. The tray on which it stands was ordered from Venetian goldsmiths in the 17th century at a cost of 99 ducats (the price of as many bulls). Other important items in the treasury are St Blaise's arms and lower leg, which are paraded round the town on St Blaise's Day. The golden filigree work on these is of great value, especially that of the right arm because of the images of saints in rectangular lozenges. Thirty such lozenges adorned the arm before the 1667 earthquake. In 1925 a tourist stole one of them while the curator's back was turned. The left hand has a story of its own. It was brought to the city by a merchant, Tomo Viciani, in 1346, but stolen and smuggled to Genoa after the 1667 earthquake. The Senate learned of the theft and sent two envoys in hot pursuit of the relic. After much sleuthing, the envoys tracked it down and returned it to Dubrovnik in 1674. As a reward their families were exempted from paying all tax for the next nine generations. St Blaise's shin bone is encased in real gold and kept behind golden net. Because so many valuable objects were housed in the treasury, the city authorities became uneasy about entrusting the security of the building to a single key. They had three separate locks made, and three separate keys, which were held by the Bishop, the churchwarden and the Rector. In order to open the door, all three had to turn their keys at the same time. The system remained unchanged for centuries.

OTHER THINGS TO SEE IN THE TREASURY

THE ADORATION OF THE MAGI: This triptych is by a 16th-century painter of the Flemish school. When Ragusan delegates went to Constantinople to hand over their tribute to the Sultan, they took this painting with them, and used it as a portable altar. Records show that the painting undertook the journey a total of 150 times.

GIFT FOR MATTHIAS CORVINUS: An extraordinary object, consisting of a small dish and jug made of gold-plated silver, decorated with creeping lizards and other Mediterranean flora and fauna. It was made as a gift for the

Central panel of the Adoration of the Magi*, once used as a travelling altarpiece on missions to the Ottomans.*

La Madonna della Seggiola, *a version of one of Raphael's most celebrated depictions of the Virgin, and one of the prized paintings in the Cathedral treasury.*

Hungarian king Matthias Corvinus, famed for his humanism and his patronage of the arts. However, he died before he could visit Dubrovnik, so the gift was never presented to him.

WOOD FROM THE HOLY CROSS: Slightly smaller than the fragment of the true cross kept in Santa Croce in Rome, this Dubrovnik piece has nevertheless been shown to be of the same origin, and is known to have been in the possession of the Papacy in the year 1000. Its history is connected with a mysterious queen Margarita, who came to Dubrovnik with her husband Stjepan, the evangeliser of Bosnia, intending to live her last days in the city. The fragment of the cross is incorporated into a beautiful crucifix made by a Dubrovnik goldsmith, Jerolim Matov, in 1536. It is the centrepiece of the treasury, straight ahead as you enter.

JESUS'S NAPPY: For a long time this was kept by nuns at the convent of St Clare, who would cut small pieces off it to give to women in childbed as protection. Miraculously these excisions restored themselves automatically, and the nappy remained permanently entire and unmutilated. After the 1667 earthquake the relic was transferred to the treasury, where it remains to this day, kept in a 16th-century silver chest.

SEATED MADONNA: Raphael painted his famous *Madonna della Seggiola* for the Medici family. The original hangs in the Palazzo Pitti in Florence. This Dubrovnik version is a copy, also said to be by the master's hand.

A Handful of Heroes

MARIN GETALDIĆ (1566–1626): Born into an aristocratic Ragusan family, Getaldić served in the Republic's government, as well as travelling extensively. It was during his travels that he fell in with a number of scientists, including Galileo, and in fact went on to become one of the leading natural philosophers and astronomers of his generation: some of his discoveries foreshadowed Newton, and he is credited with having applied geometry to algebra before Descartes. His favourite place of retreat was a cave where he would conduct experiments using reflectors to set ships on fire. The scientific world appreciated what he was trying to do; local people were not so impressed and concluded that he was a wizard.

RUĐER BOŠKOVIĆ (1711–1787):

Mathematician and natural philosopher, born into a well-to-do Dubrovnik family, members of the powerful Antunini fraternity of merchants and traders. He received a Jesuit education in Dubrovnik and Rome, and was much respected by the Vatican. It was largely thanks to Bošković that the Pope finally declared Copernicus's heliocentric theory non-heretical. Bošković also spent time in London, where he was made a fellow of the Royal Society and where he met Samuel Johnson. His success meant that he was in great demand internationally; it also fanned his natural vanity, and when in later life his reputation began to wane, he took it very hard, becoming melancholy and withdrawn. He died of pneumonia in Milan.

JOSIP STROSSMAYER (1815–1905): A lifelong campaigner for Yugoslavism: political cooperation between Croat and Serb and religious reconciliation between Catholic and Orthodox. Active in politics within the Croatian National Party, he was an instinctive federalist, opposed to Vienna-based centralism. When the Compromise Agreement of 1867 established the Dual Monarchy of Austria-Hungary, Bishop Strossmayer set about negotiating a Croatian version of the same thing (the *Nagodba*) to allow Croatia to control her own internal affairs. The terms of the agreement were never satisfactory, however, and Strossmayer retired from politics as a result.

FRANO SUPILO (1870–1917): Politician born in Cavtat, instrumental in setting up the Croato-Serb coalition in 1905, a body which wanted to end Serbo-Croat feuds and to gain greater representation within the Austro-Hungarian monarchy. Hungarian politicians thus far had encouraged quarrels among Slavs as a way of diluting their power and influence. When accused by an Austrian historian of conspiring to undermine Habsburg authority in the Balkans, Supilo sued for libel and won the case. In 1918, when the Austrian empire collapsed, so too did the strong voice of his Coalition within Croatian politics—but fortunately for Supilo, he did not live to see it happen.

ARCHITECTURE

The Englishman Thomas Watkins, visiting Dubrovnik before the French Revolution, remarked that the Ragusan citizens 'have more learning and less ostentation than any people I know'. Certainly looking round the old town it is difficult to find examples of pomp and vainglory. Most of the buildings manage to combine a modest gracefulness with a sort of functional solidity. And perhaps this was deliberate. Ruled by such a tiny aristocratic elite, Ragusa was gripped by a fear almost bordering on paranoia of allowing any member of those families to get above themselves. Monuments to great men were almost never erected. The Rector only held his position for a single month, during which time he was strictly confined to his palace, alone and without his family, lest any of the noble wives get too fond of the fine lifestyle. No one wanted a situation where one man's personal success led to overweening pride in his own achievements rather than those of his Republic. And no one wanted any of the families to become pre-eminent and establish a ruling dynasty.

Tympanum on the chapel of St Luke, carved in typical Ragusan vernacular style.

Ancient Croatian braidwork decoration on the disused chapel of SS Cosmas and Damian.

While this is undoubtedly one of the reasons for Dubrovnik's absence of florid, overblown architecture, there is another reason which is more prosaic: the great earthquake of 1667. Caught between an Ottoman empire that was beginning to flounder on the one side and a Venetian state that was ready to pounce on the other, Dubrovnik had to rebuild herself very quickly. Whereas in her 15th and early 16th century glory days, if a building was damaged she could simply build another, grander one without worrying about the cost, things were rather different in the late 17th century, and much of the rebuilding had to be done on the cheap. Compare the façades that line the Stradun with some of those that line Prijeko ulica or with those along the streets leading off Od Pustijerne, and you will notice a distinct difference between the town palaces of after the earthquake and those of before. Post-earthquake architecture is plainer; before the earthquake people were keener on visible displays of their wealth and consequence. The fact that three quarters of the city's buildings were destroyed at one fell swoop, however, does mean that the new town that rose from the rubble was an entirely homogenous and harmonious unit, and it is this that is one of the most pleasing aspects of old Dubrovnik today.

AN OVERVIEW OF STYLES

NB: Many of the buildings listed here are covered in more detail in other sections of this book. Page references are given where this is the case. The following is a brief summary of Ragusan architectural history.

THE BYZANTINE PERIOD
(9th–12th centuries)

Very little remains from this period, mainly because most buildings were made of wood, and were consumed in the great fire which devastated the town in 1296. Dubrovnik only transformed itself into the 'white city' of Gundulić's verse after 1413, when the last remaining wooden structures were demolished. Nevertheless, the old town does preserve a few secret fragments. Underneath the cathedral lie the remains of a large **Byzantine basilica**, with traces of frescoes still clearly visible. Next to the fenced-off excavation area inside the cathedral is a large black and white photograph showing wall paintings of saints and doctors of the church— sadly only their feet and the hems of their robes remain. Opposite the cathedral's west end stands the semi-tumbledown **chapel of SS Cosmas and Damian** (*map p. 199, E4*), interesting for its elaborate window frame. This kind of braided ornamentation (*pleter*) is typical of early Croatian art. Though it looks faintly Celtic, it is in fact indigenous to the Dalmatian region. Other examples can be found in chapels on the island of Koločep.

Another very early window, with rounded apertures in place of panes, is all that remains of the former **chapel of St Peter**, on the corner of Štrosmajerova and Crijevićeva (*map p. 198, C4*).

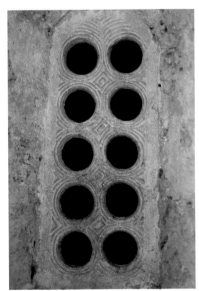

Ancient window, almost the only remnant of the ancient chapel of St Peter.

The tiny chapel of St James (Sv. Jakov) on Peline, the only surviving purely Romanesque building in the city.

ROMANESQUE & GOTHIC
(1200–1358)

Very little Romanesque architecture remains, and certainly no secular buildings, as all dwelling-houses would have been wooden structures. The grand Romanesque basilica cathedral was destroyed in the 1667 earthquake. The sole remaining purely Romanesque building in Dubrovnik is the **chapel of St James** (Sv. Jakov) on Peline (*map p. 199, D2*), at the very top of the town, in an area untouched by the 1667 tremors. Dating from 1225, it originally housed the first Dominican monks to arrive in the city. Now surrounded by buildings on all sides, it is best viewed from the city walls above.

The best Gothic structure from this period is the **Franciscan friary cloister** (1316–48), the most beautiful mediaeval cloister in Dalmatia, and possibly in Croatia as a whole (*see p. 70*). The pietà above the **south door of the Franciscan church** is another important Gothic survival (*see following page*).

THE EARLY RAGUSAN REPUBLIC
(1358–1550)

The most interesting shift that can be traced during these years of great prosperity is the tussle between the older, Venetian Gothic style and the new ideas of the Renaissance, a war which is waged on some of the city's finest façades. It is also interesting to note how many of the local masons and builders employed to execute the designs of imported Italian architects tenaciously clung to their old Gothic habits. The result is an engaging minestrone of styles—a vigorous combination of the rustic with the refined—that is entirely Ragusan. Below are the best examples:

The Rector's Palace (1464): Gothic windows on the main façade combine with a Renaissance ground-floor arcade and porch. Round the corner, overlooking Poljana Marina Držića, the windows become Renaissance as well (*map p. 199, D4*).

The Dominican Cloister (1483): Plans for a Renaissance cloister by the Florentine Maso di Bartolommeo were fairly and squarely Gothicised by the local masons who executed them, adding older-style tracery to the round Renaissance arches. The result is a lovely early experiment in eclecticism (*map p. 199, E2*).

Franciscan Church, door: This Pietà (1449, *pictured on p. 69*) by the local stonemasons the Petrović brothers is pure Gothic in style, the faces inert and mask-

Round Renaissance arches and Gothic tracery in the Dominican friary cloister: the transitional style so characteristic of Dubrovnik.

like, the clunking halos looking more like saucers, which is typical of Dalmatian sculpture of the period. The tympanum on the chapel of St Luke on Sv. Dominika (*pictured on p. 85, map p. 199, E2*) is also ascribed to the Petrović pair, though here the faces have much more character. St Luke is shown flanked by John the Baptist and St Nicholas: an engaging example of vernacular architecture. Local boys find it difficult to resist sticking cigarettes in the saints' hands. The date that is carved below them is the date that the chapel was restored.

Sponza Palace, top floors (1516–22): Dubrovnik's best example of the Gothic-Renaissance transitional style. A Renaissance porch meets Venetian Gothic ogee windows on the first floor, heading back to the Renaissance on the top storey (*pictured on p. 66*).

The Pustijerna Palaces (1550s): The area around Od Pustijerne (*map p. 199, E4*) is filled with the now derelict town palaces of the old aristocracy. Proud escutcheons adorn almost every entranceway, and Venetian-style balconies and hooded windows still give grace to many a forlorn façade. The finest palace of all is at ulica

Once-proud entrance of the Ranjina town palace in the Pustijerna district.

Restićeva No. 1. Built for the wealthy merchant and mariner Vice Skočibuha (*see p. 115*), it is the finest surviving example of pre-earthquake residential architecture. Though it has suffered many ignominies—simultaneous occupation by Jehovah's Witnesses and Satanists, who have daubed inverted crosses in the entranceway— it still stands tall and more or less proud. It was built in 1553 by the Andrijić brothers (*see p. 94*), who were working to the plans of an Italian architect. The result is four floors of pure Renaissance splendour, unfortunately difficult to appreciate because of the narrowness of the street. The old well and washing trough still survive in the entranceway.

Several centuries of Dubrovnik architecture, from Miličević's sturdy Fort St John, to the solid, provincial-style Town Hall, built in 1864, when Dubrovnik was no more than a remote outpost of the Habsburg empire.

THE LATER RAGUSAN REPUBLIC
(1550–1808)

This period, during which Dubrovnik went into her long and gradual decline, incorporates a number of shifting architectural styles, some of them uniquely Ragusan, others simply derivative:

The Stradun (after 1667): The housefronts are identical along the length of the street. Restrained, sober and dignified, they symbolise a time when Dubrovnik had neither the time nor the money to cater to individual whims.

The Church of St Blaise (1715): This is said to be a copy of the church of San Maurizio in Venice. Nicely-proportioned, it manages to dominate its surroundings without being massive (*see p. 76*).

The Jesuit Steps (1738): The work of a Roman architect—and it shows. There is something very un-Ragusan about the extravagant breadth and sweep of these steps. Most architects in Ragusa were used to working in confined spaces, and produced designs accordingly. These steps spread to a great width, forcing everything else to make way. *Map p. 199, D4.*

THE HABSBURG PERIOD
(1815–1918)

The clearest survivals from this period are the **Town Hall** (1864) next to the Rector's Palace, built to replace the Gothic-Renaissance Hall of the Great Council, destroyed by fire a few years after the Austrians assumed control of the city. The most popular legacy of the Austrians is the **Porporela**, the quay that stretches out into the water beyond Fort St John. It has a lighthouse at its tip, and also a compass, to help you get your bearings.

Evening scene on the Porporela, the long stone quay built out into the water from Fort St John by the Austrians.

A Handful of Major Architects
and their Buildings

ONOFRIO DELLA CAVA (active in Dubrovnik 1436–1443): A hydraulic engineer and architect from Naples. His best-known works are the two Onofrian fountains at either end of the Stradun, but he also had a hand in the Rector's Palace, before it was badly damaged in an ammunition explosion and remodelled by Michelozzo (*see below*). On all these projects it seems that della Cava worked in tandem with Pietro di Martino, who produced the elaborate side entrance to the Dominican church on Sv. Dominika.

MICHELOZZO MICHELOZZI (1396–1472): A Florentine, and great exponent of the early Renaissance, which he is credited with establishing as an architectural style, together with Brunelleschi and Alberti. He worked as a partner of Donatello before becoming chief architect to the Medici family in Florence, building the Medici-Riccardi palace for Cosimo de' Medici, and restoring the Palazzo Vecchio. In Dubrovnik he designed the Minčeta tower and Fort Bokar, and introduced Renaissance elements into the Rector's Palace. Because Michelozzo was in such demand at home in Italy, his packed diary never allowed to him to stay and see his Ragusan projects through to their completion. The man he left in charge, both on the Minčeta and the Rector's Palace, was Juraj Dalmatinac (d.1473), a native Dalmatian as his name suggests, but who also went by the name Giorgio Orsini, being related to the Roman Orsini family. His best-known work is Šibenik Cathedral, further up the Dalmatian coast.

PASKO MILIČEVIĆ (c.1440–1516): Municipal engineer and architect, thought to be a native of Ston. He reconstructed the old port, building the Kaše as a protection from the waves, and adding circular fortifications to the medieval forts of St Luke (Sv. Luka) and St John (Sv. Ivan) at either end of the old harbour, as well as carrying out improvements to many sections of the city walls and gates in general. He is most famous for designing the reconstruction of the Sponza Palace, which involved incorporating the original ground-floor warehouses, adding two more storeys, and enlarging the building so that it swallowed up a former side-street and goldsmith's workshop in the process. The Sponza's central atrium follows the lines of that street, hence its peculiar narrowness.

THE ANDRIJIĆ FAMILY (active in Dubrovnik in the early 16th century): Sadly the names of the Italian architects who designed some of Dubrovnik's finest buildings have been lost in the maelstrom of time, fire, earthquake, pestilence and frail human memory. One name that recurs repeatedly in connection with Dubrovnik architecture, however, is Andrijić. The Andrijić family, father Marko and sons Petar and Josip, were highly gifted stonemasons, natives of the island of Korčula, and all three of them have left their mark on the stones of Ragusa, being employed to execute the plans of the Italian architects, who came, designed, and went away again, as well as the plans of local designers. Their style marks the transition from the Gothic to the Renaissance, as can be seen by the Sponza Palace, which they built following plans by Miličević. They also built the Renaissance Skočibuha palace (*see above*), the church of the

Full view of the compact little church of the Holy Saviour (Sv. Spas), by the Andrijić brothers.

Holy Saviour (Sv. Spas, *see p. 103*) and the chapel of the Annunciation on Sv. Dominika (*map p. 199, E2*). Compare the portals of the last two, and you will notice distinct similarities: the pediment, the angels' heads and the supporting columns are very alike in both instances.

ART & MUSEUMS

Painting has always been important to Dubrovnik, and the city is proud of its artistic heritage. Not that its native output ever came close to rivalling that of Florence or Venice, but Dubrovnik can proudly take its place among the scores of other Italian and Italian-influenced states that contributed to the mainstream of European art. The richness and quality of the works that adorned the churches and palaces in Ragusa is mentioned all the way through the city's history. And if local art never approached Florentine standards, that was largely because Dubrovnik never really tried to compete. Italian masters were invited to live and work in Ragusa, and much work was purchased from them. Sadly very few of the great treasures which we must assume the city to have contained remain. Documents exist telling us that the Franciscan church possessed works by Titian and probably Caravaggio, for example, all of which perished in the great fire that followed the earthquake of 1667. It is likely that countless other similar treasures went the same way.

The Baptism of Christ *by Mihajlo Hamzić (1509), a masterpiece of the Dubrovnik School.*

THE DUBROVNIK SCHOOL

A native Dubrovnik school of painting developed in the late 15th century, producing artists of considerable skill, though sadly very little remains. Some of the artists have come down to posterity in name only, with not a single work surviving. Those whose works are known are the following:

LOVRO DOBRIČEVIĆ (c.1420–1478): Three works survive, a *Baptism of Christ* polyptych in the Dominican friary museum (dated 1448), and another, the *Virgin with Saints*, in the church at Danče (*see p. 146, Tel: 414-098 to arrange for the church to be opened*), painted almost twenty years later. Both are intensely ritualised. The wide wreath with gold angels' wings

Virgin and Child (1448), from Dobričević's Baptism of Christ *polyptych in the Dominican friary museum.*

that frames the image of the Virgin is the same in both cases. There is also a pretty St Blaise painted on wood, a fragment of an altarpiece, in the Franciscan friary museum.

VICKO LOVRIN (fl. 1509–10): The son of Dobričević, Lovrin is now known only for his altarpiece of St Michael, shown simultaneously weighing souls and battling with the devil in the form of a dragon, in the church of Our Lady of the Snows at Cavtat. In the bottom right hand corner St Nicholas is shown performing one of his most famous acts: giving gold to the three daughters of the poor man, to save them from having to go into a life of prostitution. His symbol (which has also come to represent a pawnbroker's) is usually three golden balls.

MIHAJLO HAMZIĆ (fl. 1508–16): The son of a German cannon-maker and a Dalmatian blacksmith's daughter,

Hamzić was apprenticed to Mantegna, and came to Dubrovnik in 1508. There is a polyptych by Hamzić in the Dominican friary museum, showing sad-looking saints with downcast eyes and St Stephen and St Nicholas looking rather shell-shocked. Much more approachable than this is his *Baptism of Christ*, which hangs in the Rector's Palace. Though the scene is of a wide, expansive, and in many ways impersonal landscape, the central figures of Christ and John the Baptist are focused and very intimate.

NIKOLA BOŽIDAREVIĆ (also known as Nicola Ragusano, c.1463–1517): The greatest painter of the Dubrovnik School, son of a member of Dobričević's workshop. Though he probably studied in Italy, his style seems not to have been influenced by the Renaissance at all, remaining static and heavily stylised. The saints appear against a gold background, in the late 14th and 15th-century Sienese style, though the overall character is more Byzantine than Gothic. This is in part because Ragusan patrons were notoriously conservative. A mid 16th-century painting of St Vincent (not by Božidarević) in the Dominican friary museum, for example, is truly archaic in its lineaments, and shows the extent to which painters had to ape the past to give satisfaction. Božidarević never

St Martin and the Beggar, *by Nikola Božidarević. The beggar's face reflected in St Martin's sword is popularly believed to be a self-portrait of the artist.*

went that far. His surviving works are exquisite, combining a lovely intimacy of touch with a sumptuous use of colour. Though the style is remote and iconic, he still infuses his figures with character and a hint of humanistic influence. He is known to have produced paintings for churches, for the Great and Small Council chambers, and for well-to-do private patrons. Very little survives: there is a triptych at Dance (*map p. 142, B5. Tel: 414-098 to arrange for the church to be opened*) in which he is said to have inserted his self-portrait on the sword of St Martin (*pictured on previous page*), and three other works in the Dominican friary museum (*see p. 74*).

MODERN ART

The late 19th and the 20th centuries saw a revival in Dubrovnik painting, starting with **Vlaho Bukovac** (1855–1922). Though his life spanned the first two decades of the twentieth century, Bukovac never showed leanings toward the avant garde. His early teachers were French, and although he dabbled with Impressionism, he

Example of the art of Ivo Dulčić (1916–1975).

is best known for his portraits, where he remained doggedly belle-époque in temperament, blending a mixture of rose-tinted vision with almost photographic realism. Bukovac trained at the École des Beaux Arts, and became a member of the Paris Salon in 1878, the first Croatian painter to be awarded such a distinction. He died in Prague in 1922. A gallery exists in his former house in his native Cavtat (*see p. 171*). In Dubrovnik itself he is represented by the highly sentimental St Dominic invoking divine aid to cure a green-faced child, which hangs in the Dominican church. The Museum of Modern Art also has a collection.

Interior of the serene, hieratic Račić family mausoleum, by Ivan Meštrović.

Major twentieth century Ragusan artists are **Ivo Dulčić** (1916–1975) and **Đuro Pulitika** (b. 1922). Dulčić is represented by the stained glass windows in St Blaise's church, depicting the four Evangelists and symbols of St Blaise (*see p. 77*); and by a mosaic altarpiece in the Dominican church (*see p. 74*). Đuro Pulitika's sun-soaked local scenes (the predominant colour is usually blue, the style naïve) are for sale in galleries around town: the artist still lives and works in the city and has a studio underneath the Maritime Museum. His *Holy Family* hangs in the Dominican church (*see p. 74*).

The 'Croatian Michelangelo', the sculptor **Ivan Meštrović** (1883–1962), was not born in Dubrovnik, and spent the latter part of his life in the United States. Nevertheless the town and its environs preserve at least four of his works, all of which are characterised by the purity of line and serene sense of repose which are his hallmarks. The works are a statue of St Blaise in the niche above the inner Pile gate (*pictured on p. 11*); a small, fluid statuette of the Madonna in the right-hand family shrine in the apse of the Dominican church; a bronze of a woman with a violin opposite the west door of the cathedral; and the gleaming white, half pagan-half Christian Račić family mausoleum in Cavtat (*pictured above; also see p. 171*).

MODERN ART GALLERIES

Museum of Modern Art: The artists mentioned above are all represented here. *Umjetnička Galerija, Frana Supila 23. Open Tue–Sun 10am–7pm, 10am–5pm in winter. Map p. 134, B.*

Dulčić Masle Pulitika Gallery: Small changing displays. *Drižćeva poljana 1. Open Tues–Sun 10am–1pm & 5pm–9pm. Map p. 199, E4.*

MAJOR MUSEUMS

NB: The collection of the Dubrovnik Museum is scattered at several sites across the town. All of these are dealt with separately, in the Major Sights section:

▸ *The Rector's Palace (see p. 57);*

▸ *The Franciscan friary (see p. 68);*

▸ *The Dominican friary (see p. 72)*

THE RUPE: *Rupe* means holes; and holes are the *raison d'être* of this old granary: great cavernous grain stores lined with a special mortar that moisture could not penetrate. Most of the grain was imported from inland Albania and the Crimea. At one time there were state grain stores all over the old town, including underneath the Rector's Palace, but the 16th-century Rupe is the only one that survives. Today it probably looks much the same as it always did: a great stone barn, with enormous storage wells sunk into the rock beneath. The top floor houses an ethnographic exhibition of rural life and peasant husbandry. *Od Rupa. Open Mon–Sat 9am–2pm (winter); 9am–6pm (summer). Map p. 198, B4.*

THE MARITIME MUSEUM: Housed inside Fort St John (Sv. Ivan), this two-floor museum is a must for old salts and armchair seafarers alike. The ground-floor exhibits concentrate on the heyday of the Ragusan Republic, with maps of trading routes, charts and sextants and models of old argosies, and even the cargo of knives and little metal bells that was salvaged from one of them. Upstairs comes the great age of sail and steam, with models of steamers and ocean liners built in Glasgow, Hull, Liverpool and on Teesside, and purchased by Dubrovnik. *Fort St John (Sv. Ivan). Open Tues–Sun 9am–2pm (winter) and 9am–6pm (summer). Map p. 199, F4.*

RELIGIOUS MONUMENTS

A few scattered relics of Byzantine architecture, and a single tribute to the Eastern saint Sergius, found in the name Mt Srđ, are all that survive to remind us that Dubrovnik ever had anything to do with the Eastern Christian Empire. Despite its geographical location and its early political ties with Byzantium, Dubrovnik has always acted as an outpost of the West in the Eastern world, torch-bearer for the Pope in an area dominated by Orthodoxy, and where Christian and Muslim meet.

From the 11th century onwards, Dubrovnik had an archbishop, appointed by Pope Gregory VII. Before that the Dubrovnik bishops had styled themselves archbishop, though without the unequivocal sanction of Rome. These bishops, in conjunction with pontiffs from Constantinople, had organised missionary raids into the pagan hinterland to evangelise the Slavs. Once they had adopted the new

The prominent cross on the summit of Mt Srđ above the city marks Dubrovnik as an isolated bastion of Catholicism amid Orthodoxy and Islam.

faith, however, these Slavic peoples did not all flock peaceably into the Catholic fold. The Serbs stayed close to Constantinople, and Dubrovnik, despite its own increasingly Slav population, remained Catholic. The Bosnians, on the other hand, developed a liking for heretical schism. At the end of the 12th century their ruler, Ban Kulin, rejected Catholicism for Bogomilism, a heresy which recognised the New Testament but not the Old, abjured the material world, and condoned homosexuality as a means of contraception (begetting children meant creating more matter). Fearing that this heresy would spread to Ragusa, Franciscan and Dominican friars set up religious houses in Dubrovnik in an effort to stem the flood, lending their support to the Benedictines, who had been settled on Lokrum since 1023. Bogomils who refused to recant were often traded as slaves, since recusants were not considered to have the same rights as true believers.

As Dubrovnik grew and prospered over the centuries, so its population became more hybrid. Nevertheless, official religious tolerance only stretched so far. Applications for citizenship were voted on by the Ragusan government—a two-thirds majority was needed before applications could be ratified, and religions other than Catholic were not favoured. Catholicism remained the Republic's only official religion, and not much support was lent to any other. With so many different people from so many different cultures making up a single city state—a tiny if wealthy anomaly in an Orthodox and Muslim world—the need to make these people homogenous was keenly felt. Not that Ragusa went in for forcible conversions, but no other Christian denomination was permitted to build a place of worship within the old city walls, and this law held right up until the fall of the Republic.

WHAT TO SEE

CHURCHES & CONVENTS

NB: The Franciscan and Dominican friaries, the church of St Blaise and the cathedral are dealt with separately on pp. 68–83.

The Poor Clares' Convent: The convent of St Clare was founded in 1290, and its nuns were known for their charitable works. These nuns were in charge of the state orphanage: unwanted babies would be left on the nuns' doorstep, and the nuns would take them in, arrange for them to be baptised, and care for them until they were old enough to be offered for adoption (at five years old). The orphanage was nearby in Zlatar-ićeva. A blocked-up doorway carved with the words *Cochalvit cor meu itra me* marks the place where it stood. The convent was dissolved by the French when they took over the city, and the buildings were used as a storehouse and stables.

Carved well-head in the courtyard of the former Poor Clares' convent.

In its heyday Ragusa contained over thirty churches, and eight monasteries and convents within the city walls. The reason convents were so numerous was because the noble families provided dowries only for the eldest daughter; all remaining girls were packed off to nunneries at around the age of fourteen.

Today St Clare's nunnery courtyard functions as a restaurant in the summertime. *Poljana Paska Miličevića. Map p. 198, B3.*

The Church of the Holy Saviour (Sveti Spas): This small church was built as a votive offering to commemorate the victims of the earthquake of 1520. According to an anonymous chronicler, the earthquake was not all bad, for 'the shock caused much spiritual benefit': a rush of almsgiving ensued, and queues formed outside the confessionals. Noblemen and their wives personally lent a hand with the building of Sv. Spas, and apocryphal legends even grew up asserting that the mortar holding the masonry together had been mixed with the breastmilk of Ragusan mothers, making it exceptionally strong. This was given as one of the reasons for the church's survival of the much greater earthquake of 1667.

Three nobles were appointed to oversee the construction of the church and to regulate its cost. They succeeded as brilliantly as committees always do, managing to produce an expensive building extremely slowly—possibly, as some sharp tongues claimed, because they kept taking the stonemasons off the job to work on their own private palaces. Whether this is true or not, it hardly matters now, for the resulting building is highly distinctive and rather beautiful, some say reminiscent of the church of the Madonna dei Miracoli in Venice. We do not know for certain who the architect was, though he is more than likely to have been Italian. The stonemason in charge was a Dalmatian: Petar Andrijić (*see p. 94*). The church interior is simple, with plain ribbed vaulting and an altarpiece of Dubrovnik with St Blaise and Christ the Redeemer, into whose keeping the city is commended. *Stradun. Map p. 198, B2.*

The Serbian Orthodox Church: Until almost the end of the 19th century, Serbian Orthodox worshippers held their services in a church outside the city. In 1877, perhaps partly as a result of lifelong campaigning by Bishop Strossmayer (*see p. 84*), a new church was built for them within the old town precinct. The Orthodox Church of the Annunciation is large and lofty, built in a neo-Byzantine idiom, surrounded by a tall railing behind which lurk large numbers of hungry cats, for whom the local ladies put out scraps. The church interior preserves its wooden floor and fittings and coffered ceiling. The iconostasis is of Greek make. Above it is a large frieze of the Last Supper, with the Baptism of Christ to the left, and the Annunciation to the right. Despite the church's size, its congregation is rather small—and considering recent political events in the region, it is unlikely to grow in the foreseeable future. *Od Puča 10. Map p. 198, C3.*

The Jesuit Church: The architectural conjunction of this church, the Jesuit Steps that lead to it, and the Jesuit College that adjoins it, leaves one in no doubt that the Jesuits intended to make an impact on the city, and had no intention of confining their architecture to modest Ragusan

The Jesuit Church (1725).

building work took so long was because it was interrupted by the great earthquake (*see p. 24*) soon after it began. It seems that the Jesuits were undeterred, and that they did not interpret the quake as an inauspicious omen. Work was resumed in 1699.

The entranceway is imposing, with a double tier of Corinthian columns, and its interior is dominated by enormous side altars, two made of real marble, with *trompe l'oeil* pillars and altar surrounds. All have *trompe l'oeil* gilded tesserae (mosaic tiles) on the ceilings and around the sides. They are the work of a Spanish artist, Gaetano García. Above the main altar the apotheosised St Ignatius Loyola glides heavenward on a cotton-wool cloud, while God, Christ and the Holy Spirit wait to greet him, holding out an immortal crown. To the right of the main door is a late 19th-century model of the grotto at Lourdes, lit with natural light, where a supplicant kneels before a blue-robed Virgin, her crutch cast optimistically aside.

proportions. Seen from almost any vantage point, the Jesuit church looks massive: its great buttressed sides heave themselves far above the line of the surrounding roofs and city walls. The church was built between 1667 and 1725 by Andrea Pozzo—a Jesuit himself, and one of the Society's most prominent Baroque architects. This was his first commission outside Rome, though not his last. Later he went on to design the cathedral in Ljubljana and the magnificent Jesuit church in Vienna. The reason the

A number of Dubrovnik's noted men of science and letters were the products of the Jesuit College, among them Ruđer Bošković and Ivan Gundulić (*see pp. 84 & 132*). On the seaward side of the building, visible from the city walls, is an enormous version of the emblem IHS, the encrypted, vowelless form of the name Jesus, which because the Jesuits are the Society of Jesus, has become associated with them as their badge. IHS is an extremely common feature of buildings in Dubrovnik, and though not all instances of it are Jesuit-linked, no building which has ever had a Jesuit connection will be without it. *Poljana Ruđera Boškovića. Open 8am–12.30 and 4pm–6.30pm. Map p. 198, C5.*

THE SYNAGOGUE & MOSQUE

The Synagogue: The first Jewish families arrived in Dubrovnik at the end of the 13th and the beginning of the 14th centuries. They lived freely in the community, and no systematic discrimination appears to have been practised, nor do they appear to have minded the idea of assimilation. Total harmony between Jew and Christian never reigned, though. When the plague first broke out in 1348, it was widely and maliciously rumoured that the Jews had poisoned the wells. There is no evidence of outright persecution, however, and in 1407 the Jews were accorded the precious and much sought-after status of Ragusan citizens, permitted to reside within the city walls. They were also allowed to build a place of worship, a favour accorded to no other non-Catholic group until after the fall of the Ragusan Republic in 1808. Dubrovnik's little synagogue, which dates from the 15th century, is one of the oldest in Europe. When Ferdinand and Isabella expelled the Jews from Spain in 1492, many of them found sanctuary in Dubrovnik, swelling the small community to the extent that tensions grew between Jew and Christian. Jews found themselves exposed to charges of ritual murder. In view of the strained relations, the Dubrovnik authorities decided to contain the Jewish population, confining them to an enclosed ghetto. In 1540 a distinct Jewish area was created, around today's ulica Žudioska, which had a gate at either end. Hebrew blessings are carved above a number of the windows in this street. Though the Dubrovnik Jewish community numbers only forty today (in the 17th century it numbered some 250), the synagogue is still in use and preserves its original 17th-century furniture. It is a Sephardic foundation—the old list of earthquake victims on display in the

Interior of Dubrovnik's Sephardic synagogue, situated in the main street of the former old town ghetto.

walls, to which there was direct access from the surrounding houses, and watch the services from behind the slatted screens. These chambers are said to have been used as hiding places for the synagogue treasures when the Nazis occupied the town in 1943. Twenty-seven Dubrovnik Jews died in the Holocaust. *Žudioska 3. Open Mon–Fri 10am–1pm. Map p. 199, D3.*

The Mosque: Muslims in Dubrovnik only began to form an organised community in the early decades of the 20th century. Today they have a permanent place of worship, richly draped in rugs, housed in a first-floor apartment in an old patrician mansion in the heart of the old town. To visit the mosque, you will be expected to remove your shoes. Special shoe racks are provided outside the door. *Miha Pracata 3. Open 10am–1pm; Thursdays 5pm–7pm. Map p. 198, C4.*

small museum on the first floor features predominantly Spanish names. Women now sit on the balcony. In former times they would enter special chambers behind the

PART III

GUIDED WALKS

Each of these walks is designed to take between 45 minutes to an hour. By visiting the museums, churches, cafés or restaurants that are included along the way, you can make them last a whole morning or afternoon. The exception is Walk Four, which is twice as long as the others, and can be divided into two sections: from the Ploče Gate to the Hotel Excelsior, Hotel Argentina and Villa Dubrovnik, and from those hotels to the former monastery of St James (Sv. Jakov), with its pretty beach.

Key streets and sights are marked in bold throughout.

p. 111 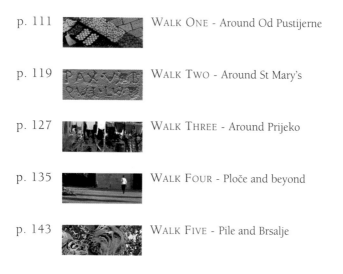 WALK ONE - Around Od Pustijerne

p. 119 WALK TWO - Around St Mary's

p. 127 WALK THREE - Around Prijeko

p. 135 WALK FOUR - Ploče and beyond

p. 143 WALK FIVE - Pile and Brsalje

Doorway on Ilije Sarake, behind the cathedral.

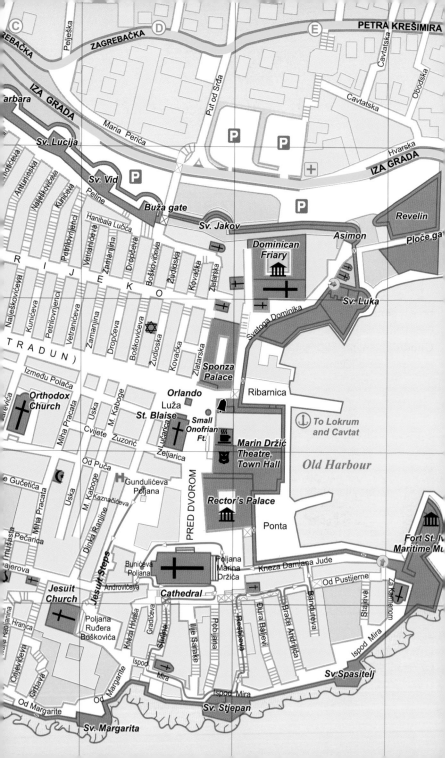

AROUND OD PUSTIJERNE

The street name Od Pustijerne is a corruption of the Latin post terra, meaning an area outside the main settlement. This ancient former suburb was popular with wealthy 16th-century Ragusans as the site for their town palaces.

This walk begins in the centre of **Gundulićeva poljana**, a broad, sunny square dominated by the 19th-century **statue of Ivan Gundulić** (*see p. 132*), not only the greatest poet of Dubrovnik, but also one of the founding fathers of Croatian literature itself, whose bewigged image adorns the 50 kn note. Around his feet the market ladies set up their stalls of dried figs, lavender oil and fresh fruit and vegetables. The square also plays host to a couple of good café restaurants, popular with the market people for an early morning coffee, and good places to stop for a quick lunch of salad and seafood risotto. In the middle of day corn in thrown for the

Market stalls on Gundulićeva poljana.

square's pigeons: instantly the whirr of hundreds of eager wing-beats fills the air.

Behind Gundulić stands a small fountain, put up for public use in 1902 by one of the Amerlings, an Austro-Hungarian family whose name you will see cropping up on plaques all over town commemorating their numerous acts of social munificence. The bowl of this fountain was completely shattered in the 1991–92 war. Now restored, you can hardly tell that it is a reconstruction.

Leaving the Gundulić statue behind you, head out of the square towards a broad, balustraded stairway. These are the **Jesuit steps**, the work of a Roman architect, built in 1738 as an appropriately awe-inspiring ascent to the enormous (by Ragusan proportions) Jesuit church and college at the top (*see p. 104*). The Jesuit arrival in town was not achieved without a certain amount of local resistance. Though the Ragusan clergy were impressed by their excellence as teachers, the Ragusan Senate was worried by their implacable anti-Ottoman stance, and feared that political tensions might result. The Jesuit mission went ahead, though, and some of their zeal rubbed off on their most famous pupil, Ivan Gundulić, who is said to have become intensely prelatical in later life,

burning most of his early works, which he had come to regard as embarrassingly frivolous. In fact his most famous poem, *Osman*, is highly critical of Ottoman corruption and of Islam in general. Because of this it was never published in Gundulić's lifetime. The authorities tactfully decided to duplicate it in manuscript copy only. The pious Jesuit fathers themselves would be spinning in their coffins if they knew that not many years ago their magnificent flight of steps had been used as the backdrop to a local beauty contest, all the lovelies being required to trip down them in their bikinis and high heels to show off their perfect posture and their secular statistics.

Don't climb all the way to the top of the steps, but turn left into Androvićeva, then through Bunićeva poljana at the bottom, and, walking alongside the cathedral, take the second flight of steps to your right, turning right at the top of them, and into a little square. You are overlooked as you do so by the statue of St Mark, accompanied by his lion emblem, on the cathedral roof. The other three Evangelists are placed on the other side, facing the Rector's Palace; only Mark has been relegated to the back; perhaps a subtle snub to the great patron saint of rival Venice. Local tradition makes no comment.

Pass under the archway now, and then immediately left into ulica Stulina. Here you are in one of the most ancient enclaves of the town, its street layout dating back to the days when the Stradun was still a watery channel. This street is mentioned by the Byzantine emperor Constantine Porphyrogenitus as the site of the 10th-century **church of St Stephen** (Sv. Stjepan), the church where Canon Stoico was at prayer when St Blaise appeared to him in a vision warning of Venetian attack (*see p. 11*). After a second archway, at the point where the street turns sharp right you will see two ancient doorways. On the right is a door with a blocked up balustrade above it and the coat-of-arms of the Gradić family (a stairway).

Straight ahead is a boarded-up doorway and a fallen column. Behind the door lie the ruins of the church. Go round the dogleg of the street and peer in through the boarded-up west entrance, and you can glimpse them amid the brambles and the locust trees. Turn left where the street forks, following a sign to the Konoba Ekvinocijo. The street brings you out right under the city walls. Go straight on, leaving the Ekvinocijo on your left. A door in the walls on your right leads to a flight of steps going down to a bathing place. 'No Toples, No Nudist' says a painted admonition on the wall to your left. To your right is a little glass-painted icon of St Stephen, a clear reminder that his church once stood here, and above

Peeping through the boarded-up doorway of the ancient church of St Stephen.

the doorway itself is carved the legend *Vrata S. Stjepana*—St Stephen's Gate.

Follow the street, Ispod Mira, as it curves round to the left and then turn right, still hugging the city walls, turning left between a faded pink building and a ramshackle wooden doorway into ulica Restićeva. Passing under an archway, look above and behind, and you will see a stone tablet proclaiming this as the site of Dubrovnik's first children's home, set up by one of the philanthropic Amerlings. At **Restićeva No. 1** stands a magnificent, collapsing Renaissance palace, its proportions and its splendour not well served by the narrowness of the street, which makes it difficult to view and appreciate properly, and which has also forced it to develop upwards rather than outwards (it is only one room deep). In fact the best vantage point from which to view the house is the city walls, from where you gain a real impression of its size relative to its surroundings. It is the former town mansion of the great seafaring Skočibuha family, whose accumulated wealth allowed them to aspire to a lifestyle not dissimilar to that of the noble families, though they were of commoner stock themselves

Families of cats now hold court in the derelict palaces of old Ragusan noblemen.

(their name, rather ignobly, translates as 'hopping flea'). The house is a superb example of pre-earthquake Ragusa architecture. It was built in 1553, following plans by an architect from Padua, by the Andrijić brothers (*see p. 94*), who were employed on a number of architectural projects in this area.

At the end of Restićeva, turn right. Go under the archway, and on your left you will see the tiny derelict chapel of SS Cosmas and Damian. Abutting it is a ruined palace. Its doorway has the Sorkočević coat of arms above it—this, perhaps, was the very building from the whose window the unhappy composer Luka Sorkočević threw himself to his death in 1789 (*see p. 140*). Continue up the street now, past more forlorn palaces, until you come to ulica Braće Andrijića, the street named after the stonemason brothers, where at No. 10 you will see another example of their handiwork, the Venetian Gothic former mansion of the noble Ranjina family. Their Italian name means spider, hence the three arachnids on their coat of arms. This area of town was once filled with the palaces of the ruling oligarchs—the Skočibuhas had definitely chosen an upmarket milieu to move in—but almost without exception those palaces are deserted and crumbling today, with families of

The 16th-century town residence of the Skočibuha family, the finest example of secular Renaissance architecture remaining in the city.

stray cats occupying their former silk-hung halls and Romeo-and-Juliet balconies, although the proud patrician escutcheons still stare out at you from above the entranceways, announcing who was once to be found at home here. The dereliction of this part of town is not a consequence of the most recent war but of the 1979 earthquake. Plans to buy out 700 locals and turn the whole district into a tourist complex of holiday apartments and pizzerias were thankfully shelved, but no alternative plan to regenerate the area and save the surviving buildings has so far been forthcoming.

The next street, **Bandureva**, also contains its fair share of escutcheons, this time of the Bunić (Bona) and Kaboga (Caboga) families. These two noble names were eventually linked by marriage, but they have something else in common, too, in that they produced two of the most celebrated emissaries (*poklisari*) of the Ragusan Republic, Marojica Kaboga and Nikolica Bunić (*see p. 61*).

Turn left across the cobbled courtyard now, and down the flight of steps into Kneza Damjana Jude. Turn left at the bottom, going past the carpenter's workshop that makes the sets and props for the Marin Držić Theatre, to emerge opposite the cathedral. Leaving the cathedral to your left, enter **Bunićeva poljana**, the square named in honour of the great doomed diplomat (his ladder-and-eagle coat of arms adorns many of the façades), where a variety of cafés and bars competes for your attention, notably the Troubadour, whose owner, a musician, can be seen playing the double bass here in the evenings. Alternatively, if you prefer to sit by the sea, turn right up Kneza Damjana Jude and through the little archway in the wall on your left—opposite the Miho Pracat Mariners' Club, where the seadogs sit with their newspapers—which takes you into the old port.

WALK TWO

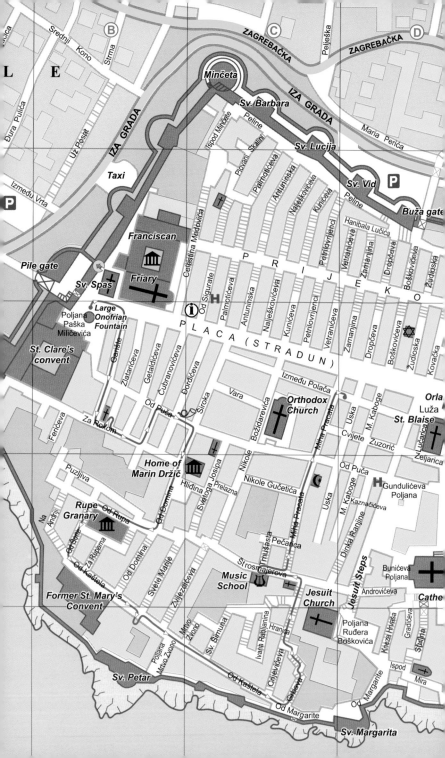

AROUND ST MARY'S

The former convent of St Mary stands in the very oldest part of the old town, surrounded by a warren of winding narrow streets, tucked just below the city walls, and close to the former state grain store.

This walk begins beside the large Onofrian fountain (*see p. 53*). Behind it stretches the former **convent of St Clare**. Dissolved in 1808, the convent was, in its mediaeval heyday, the site of much of the town's charitable work. The poorhouse and hospice stood nearby, and the Poor Clares also undertook to see that all the unwanted babies deposited anonymously on their doorstep were safely housed in the Republic's orphanage. All foundlings were cared for here until the age of five, when they were put up for adoption. The same nuns also had the safekeeping of a miraculous piece of cloth, reputed to be a nappy worn by the infant Jesus (*see p. 82*).

Make-believe mediaeval minstrel entertains passers-by beside the large Onofrian fountain.

With your back to the Onofrian fountain, set off down the Stradun, turning almost immediately right, through an archway, into Garište. Archways linking the upper floors of buildings in this way were relatively common in the pre-earthquake city. During the fire that raged through the town after the earthquake of 1667, such arches made it easier for the flames to leap from building to building: compounded with a stiff spring wind they turned whole streets into lethal fire corridors, which is why they are a relatively rare feature of post-earthquake Dubrovnik architecture. The name of this street, Garište, literally means 'burnt area', and was the name given to the whole of this former suburb of the original town. It got its name from a much earlier fire, that of 1296, which licked its way hungrily through the old wooden-built city.

At the end of Garište, turn left into Za Rokom, which takes its name from the church immediately on your left, the **church of St Roch**, patron saint of the plague-stricken. Duck down the street on the other side of the church and beyond the blocked-up doorway look for the Latin graffiti on the side wall of the church, dated 1597: *Ego vos animadverto ludentes* . . . 'I'm warning you, ball-players. Peace be with you, but remember that you will die'. Evidently the words of a local resident in desperate need of some peace and quiet, driven to distraction by the children playing ball in the street—something they do to this day.

Coming back to Za Rokom, turn left and second left again down Ćubranovićeva, which brings you out onto **Od Puča**. In former days this was the street where the city wells were situated, yielding bucketfuls of brackish water before Onofrio della Cava's aqueduct and lead-piping system brought a clean, constant supply in the 15th century. Today the street is a busy thoroughfare of shops and old-fashioned barbers and

Mediaeval graffiti on the side wall of the church of St Roch.

Jeweller's display window on ulica Od Puča, where gold and silversmiths cluster.

jewellers selling traditional silver filigree-ware, notably at this Ćubranovićeva corner—appropriate since Ćubranović himself was a goldsmith before he metamorphosed into a poet of Italianate carnival ditties and masques.

Turn right, past more jewellers, and when you come to Široka, turn right. At No. 7 on the left you will find the former home of the comic playwright and champion of the common man **Marin Držić** (*see p. 132*). His house is now a museum, but don't be beguiled by the tourist leaflets promising you a trip back in time to the 16th century. The furthest back the museum will take you is 1967, when it was set up. But for serious enthusiasts, cassette guides are available in English, and you can see the undercroft beneath the house, from which Držić had his own private access to the **Church of All Saints** (popularly known as the Domino church) next door. How sedulous a member of the congregation he was is not known, though he had every reason to be keen, as he somehow owned the rights to part of the church's revenue. Dire financial difficulties in later life induced him to sell these rights for cash, whereupon he took himself to Venice, and died there, alone and embittered, having failed in his cherished ambition to topple the Ragusan oligarchs from their perch.

Inserted sideways into the outer wall of the Domino church is a tablet dedicated to the *Confraternità dei Muratori*: the guild of stonemasons. Note the mortar trowel and set squares depicted in their emblem. During the days of the Ragusan Republic, the Dubrovnik craftsmen were organised into confraternities and guilds—twenty-one of them in all—which had their spiritual home at one or other of the city churches.

Continue up the street now, going up the steps past the Steak House Domino, climbing steadily until you come to ulica Od Rupa, at which point turn right. This brings you out onto a broad, flat terrace just outside the **Rupe**, the old town granary and now a museum (*see p. 100*), with good views out across the ancient roofs and roof-terraces garlanded with creeping vines and drying laundry, with the city walls beyond, sweeping upwards to the massive Minčeta tower, and the Franciscan church stretching away up the line of the Stradun.

Alongside the further end of the Rupe, go left up Od Šorte, noting the emblem of St Peter and the crossed keys carved as a talisman over the

Entranceway to the former convent of St Mary, now used as residential flats.

doorways to Nos. 3 and 7. At the top of the street, if you look to your right, you will see the suburb of Pile, dominated by the 19th-century bulk of the Hotel Hilton Imperial. Turn left, walking under the lee of an austere, barracks-like building, the former Benedictine **convent of St Mary**, dissolved by Napoleon's men. The reason it looks so much like a barracks is because the French troops turned it into one, installing a military hospital on the same site. Today it has become a warren of ramshackle private dwellings. At ulica Svete Marije you will see the main entranceway, up to your right. Its tympanum shows the Angel Gabriel appearing to Mary, above which hang the coats of arms of Dubrovnik itself, plus those of all the noble families who endowed the convent—and presumably plonked their surplus daughters within its sombre walls. Going up the old steps, trodden shallow and sloping by centuries of feet, you come into a dilapidated courtyard. Even the old convent church has been turned into flats.

Leave the convent now and continue to your right up Od Kaštela. The street takes its name from the Latin word *castellum*, a fortress or citadel. This is the area that was first settled by refugees from Epidaurum in the 7th century. Old maps show a little walled enclave huddled up on this jutting corner of rock. The citadel itself was demolished in 1150, and the convent took its place. Today, as well as being the most ancient part of town, this is also one of the poorest, although a certain amount of building and home-improvement is going on. Continue until you come to the little plateau-like square of **Poljana Mrtvo Zvono** (Dead Bell Square). The place gets its name from the bell that was once tolled near here to announce an execution or an exile. You are now right up against the city walls. Further on, to your right, past a pair of

lovingly-tended vegetable gardens, you will see people walking along the walls overhead. The area looks pretty on a sunny day, but on wild late winter afternoons, when the Yugo wind blows in from off the sea, it can seem a very desolate spot indeed, just the place where a death knell might toll. The southerly Yugo is famous in Dubrovnik. During the days of the Republic it was commonly acknowledged that it had an adverse effect on people's mental balance, and sessions of the Senate would be suspended until it blew itself out. If you were convicted of a crime, and could prove that the Yugo was blowing when you committed it, that would be regarded as an extenuating circumstance and you could expect to get off with a lighter sentence. On Yugo days, the macabre front-step garden of mesembryanthemums, artificial flowers and plastic dolls' heads on spikes on the corner of Grbava looks very sinister indeed, like something out of a cautionary tale.

The wooden sign for 'Cold Drinks' in front of you leads to the Buža bar (*see p. 180*)

Turn down Grbava now, looking out for the inscription above the entrance to No 1 (after the first left turn): *Si deus pro me quis contra me*: 'If God is for me, who is against me?' This narrow, winding, ripe-smelling street plunges steeply down, back into the bowels of the old town. Your descent might be accompanied by the sound of piano playing or violins, and if it is, you will soon see why. Just before an archway at the end of the downward spiral, look to your left to note an ancient decorated window with round apertures in place of panes, the only remnant of the 10th-century **chapel of St Peter**. Go under the archway and turn left. On your left you will find the source of the piano-playing, the **Dubrovnik Music School**, named after the 18th-century Ragusan composer Luka Sorkočević (*see p. 140*), and housed in the former nunnery of St Catherine of Siena. Above the inner entrance-way is an old tympanum with carved saints and the former nunnery name. The outer, street entrance shows Christ flanked by saints, one of whom is St Peter with his keys, a reminder of the ancient chapel, now in ruins and barely visible, to your left. Today concerts are regularly held in the Music School courtyard.

Carry on downwards now, along Miha Pracata, a street that is typically filled with children burdened with guitars and violin cases, hurrying to and from their music lessons. The street was formerly known as Pucić Street after the family whose fleur-de-lis-embossed escutcheon hangs over so many of the doorways, including that of the little chapel of St Vitus on the right-hand side as you descend. A few doors down from the chapel, at No. 3, another noble patrician mansion has given over some of its floor space to the **Dubrovnik mosque** (*see p. 107*). Further along still, on the corner of Između Polača, the Karaka tavern offers a rest and good cheer. Being named after the biggest and most famous of all the Ragusan merchant vessels, the carrack, you will not be surprised to find that the place has a nautical theme, including, in one of its nooks (visible from the street window), a copy of the portrait of the mariner Skočibuha (*see p. 36*). What might seem more incongruous about it is its branding as an Irish pub—but Guinness lovers should be delighted. It is one of only two bars in Dubrovnik which stays open into the small hours.

Maro and Baro, the bronze figures who strike the hours in Dubrovnik's clocktower belfry.

WALK THREE

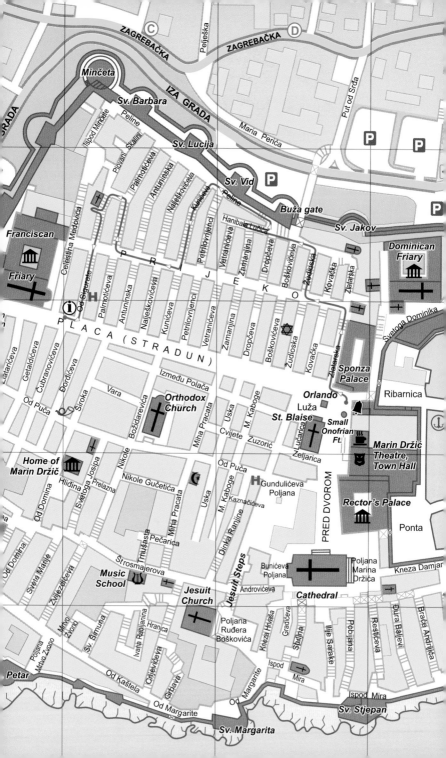

AROUND PRIJEKO

The streets that climb up the hill to the north of the Stradun were once home to Dubrovnik's craftsmen and merchants. NB: this walk involves a lot of up-and-down climbing.

This walk begins in Luža, the broad square at the head of the Stradun, underneath the **city clocktower**, where the *Zelenci*, the 'green men' Maro and Baro, hammer out the hours as they have done since the 15th century when the tower was built. The clocktower dates from 1929, a reconstruction of a much earlier tower. The digital clock in the stem is much easier to read than the elaborate single-hand clockface above it. To the left of the clocktower stands the old **city belltower**, again not as old as it might appear. It is a 1952 reproduction of the 15th-century original, which was altered in the 19th century to incorporate a first-floor apartment for the Austrian governor. To the right of the clocktower are the

Colourful laundry hung out to dry amid the greenery above Prijeko.

Prijeko, Dubrovnik's street of restaurants, with the church of St Nicholas at the end.

former **headquarters of the City Guard**, with a head in a plumed helmet, cannon and cannon balls over the entrance. The building dates from the same time as St Blaise's church, and is by the same architect. The City Guard consisted of a standing force of 127 men drawn by lot every month from among the citizenry. Extra recruits were brought in in times of emergency or danger.

With the clock tower behind you, turn right up Zlatarska, pausing to note the old-fashioned bell-pull at No. 1. At the corner of Prijeko, on your right, is the little **church of St Nicholas** (Sv. Nikola), where local choral societies rehearse in the evenings, making a meal on the terrace of the next-door Rozarij restaurant very pleasant indeed. The restaurant is named after the nearby church of the Rosary, attached to the Dominican friary complex. St Dominic is said to have invented the rosary beads.

Turn left now, along Prijeko. The name roughly translates as 'beyond street' or 'other side street': the thoroughfare is so termed because it once lay on the farther bank of the salt-water creek (now the Stradun) which separated the Latin town from the mainland Slavic town. This warren of high, narrow, clambering streets, full of plants and drying laundry, was once a busy area of artisans' workshops and craftsmen's houses, to which the street names still bear witness: Zlatarska: Goldsmith Street, Kovačka: Blacksmith Street, and Peline, above Prijeko, whose name comes from a corruption of the word for skinner or furrier. Nowadays the artisans have almost all gone, and the clang of hammer against anvil has been replaced by the amplified beats emanating from all the bars that infest the area, to the torment of local residents trying to sleep. In the days of mass tourism Prijeko reinvented itself as Dubrovnik's main restaurant alley. The touts employed to lure you to a table can sometimes become too much, and sadly very few of the restaurants are hand-on-heart recommendable.

Turn right up **Žudioska**, Jew Street, the original street of the mid 16th-century Jewish ghetto. This ghetto was enclosed by gates which were locked at night and unlocked first thing in the morning by the official designated to keep the keys. The houses in the street, which consisted of storerooms and workshops below and living quarters above, were all subject to a fixed rent. Below you at No. 3 is the synagogue, still in use today by the tiny Jewish community that remains

Menorah etched into a doorway on Žudioska ulica.

(*see p. 106*). Above you is a world of intense light and shade, the narrow streets always in shadow, the sky a bright slit above your head. As you climb higher you come upon traces of ancient masonry, with a particularly fine remnant at No. 20. St Peter the heavenly doorkeeper sits above the lintel with his keys. Above him are fine Gothic windows with scrollwork and billeted hoods. This higher section of the town, along with its elevated counterpart on the other side of the Stradun, suffered less heavily in the 1667 earthquake, and more ancient fragments remain.

At the top of Žudioska you come out into the highest street in this part of town, Peline, which runs directly beneath the city walls. To your right the tower of the Dominican church rears into the sky. Turn left and walk for a few yards. To your right are the city walls, and the **Buža gate** (literally the 'hole in the wall'), the newest of the city gates, constructed in 1908. In the evenings ulica Boškovićeva, into which it leads, becomes a regular thoroughfare as people leave their cars outside the walls and walk through Buža and down to the Stradun for a night out. On the corner just before Buža, the

Zlatni Puder snack bar sells cheese, potato and spinach *burek* made with filo pastry brought from Sarajevo.

Straight ahead of you the streets fork. To your left is a splendid, almost vertical view down **Dropčeva** into the bright white sunlit Stradun, the view filtered through a confused lens of flapping underwear, rubber-plant leaves, and shop and café lanterns. Dropčeva takes its name from the 19th-century pharmacist Antun Drobac, who had a chemist's shop on the Stradun (still a chemist's today), and who invented pyrethrum powder, an insecticide obtained from tansy flowers, and a breakthrough in its day.

Take the left fork. The street you enter now is named after the late 15th-century magistrate-turned-love-lyricist Hannibal Lučić, who wrote fervent sonnets in the Petrarchan manner. Peer to your left down Zamanjina and you will see the tiny chapel of St Vitus, with its pretty moulded doorway and miniature belfry. The celebrated Dubrovnik artist Đuro Pulitika (*see p. 99*) lives and works in this street. Don't turn down it, but retrace your steps to Peline. Walk on for a little way, then turn left down Kunićeva, the prettiest of all these streets. When you pass No. 24 on your left, look upwards to see the **last will and testament** of Andrija Valcovich (1728) set into the wall between the top-floor windows in the form of a stone tablet, announcing to the world at large that he leaves his worldly goods to his daughter, who looked after him in life and whom he hopes will remember him in death.

The protruding stone struts with holes pierced in them, a feature of so many houses here, and now used for suspending washing lines, were originally for drying skeins of woollen and silken yarn—Dubrovnik was famous for its textiles. To ensure that neighbours living in such close proximity to each other had at least a modicum of privacy, a law was incorporated into the 1272 city statute stating that no two windows should look directly in on one another. The same statute also stipulated that all balconies must be high enough to allow a woman with a laden basket on her head to pass underneath.

As you get nearer to **Prijeko**, you will notice how the houses get larger and finer. Prijeko itself was home to wealthy and successful merchants and mariners. Turn right. The façades that stand diagonally opposite each other at Nos. 23 and 24 give an idea of the style in which these people lived. The former, on the left, has an upper-floor balcony supported by lions and a female head. The companion head (perhaps a male one) has fallen off. Slightly further up on the right, at No. 24, the entranceway is flanked by two carved centaurs, with a splendid balcony above, shaded by an ancient vine trained from pavement level, its lower trunk protected by a wooden surround.

For an impression of what these town houses would once have looked like inside, pop up to the first floor of the **Restaurant Antunini** at No. 30. During the days of the Republic, Ragusa's merchants and craftsmen were all organised into a system of different confraternities and guilds, which conferred social and commercial benefits on members, but which also had a quasi-religious function, aiming to promote piety and charity among the population. The wealthiest and most powerful of these confraternities were the Lazarini—whose members were chiefly merchants who traded with the Levant—and the Antunini, whose members traded with western centres. With its red silk walls and gilt-framed mirrors, the Antunini restaurant does a good job of recreating the kind of living room that one such merchant family might have boasted.

Go up Palmotićeva now (just before the Antunini), then turn left opposite No. 18. Turn left again at the first fork, and at No. 13 on your right you will find the entrance (with a fig tree growing out of it) to the well-concealed convent **Chapel of the Transfiguration** (Sigurata). The church is of very ancient foundation. Though what you see now is 17th century, it was originally built to serve an adjoining Franciscan nunnery. It was also the seat of the guild of blacksmiths, which is why a couple of the old tombstones in the yard (at the foot of the broad steps) have stylised anvils on them.

Continue your descent to the Stradun now, where the Festival Café awaits with a cool glass of Ožujsko beer, or maybe coffee and a slice of gateau.

View from Peline at the top of the town.

Literary Ragusans

At the beginning of the 19th century the Croatian romantic writer Ljudevit Gaj issued a cry of 'cultural patriotism', calling for the history and literature of his fatherland to be 'lifted out of the miserable Magyar darkness'. He came up against a great stumbling block though: language. In what language was the great new canon of national literature to be written? The Dalmatian aristocrats spoke Italian. The educated classes in Slavonia used Latin for official business and often spoke German or Hungarian at home. The various forms of Croatian were largely vernacular dialects spoken by the peasantry—except perhaps the Štokaski dialect, the language of the great Gundulić (*see below*), and the language of Dubrovnik. Dubrovnik at that time had something of a cult status in Croatia as a bastion of native Slav culture, a symbol of liberty and independence from Turkish, Hungarian and Austrian domination. 16th-century Ragusan plays were all the rage in the literary salons of Zagreb—and the fashion endured until the end of the 19th century.

IVAN GUNDULIĆ (1589–1638): The poet Gundulić is Dubrovnik's greatest writer and a symbol of Croatian national identity. When the new Croatian National Theatre was built in Zagreb in the late 19th century, its stage curtain was adorned with an image of Gundulić enthroned, entitled 'Croatian Renaissance', and painted by the Dubrovnik artist Vlaho Bukovac (*see p. 98*). While the language of Gundulić was adopted as the language of Croatia as a whole, his passionate lyrics extolling freedom were raised to anthem status. Born into a prominent noble family, Gundulić was twice elected Rector of Konavle, widely seen as a sort of rector-in-waiting post for Dubrovnik itself, though he died too young ever to hold that august position (Dubrovnik rectors had to be at least fifty). One of the only famous Ragusans to have a monument erected in his memory, his periwigged statue dominates Gudulićeva poljana, and the statue's plinth is decorated with scenes from his most famous poem, *Osman*, which tells of the defeat of the Turkish Sultan by the Polish army, and which contains his famous description of Dubrovnik as the 'white city'.

MARIN DRŽIĆ (1508–1567): Many of the 16th-century plays performed in the fashionable Zagreb salons were probably the work of Držić. His comedies are still performed today—and though he is often compared to Molière because of certain similarities in his plots and characters, he in fact predates Molière by more than a century. Although Držić maintained a stance that was antagonistic to the ruling elite, his work was so popular that he came to no harm. We do not know if any of the nobles saw the funny side in constantly being portrayed as a class of blithering inbred idiots deservedly outwitted by their canny, streetwise servants; but even if they didn't, Držić was never clapped in irons, not even when he began actively plotting to overthrow the Ragusan government system. No success ever crowned his revolutionary intrigues, and in later life he left Dubrovnik for Venice, where he died in poverty. The house where Držić lived is now a museum. *Dom Marina Držića, Široka 7. Open 9am–2pm. Map p. 198, C4.*

The solitary church of Sv. Jakov Višnjica.

WALK FOUR

PLOČE & BEYOND

The tree-shaded stretch of seaside road between the suburb of Ploče and the former monastery of Sv. Jakov Višnjica makes a perfect early evening stroll. If you are staying at one of the hotels along the way, you can join the walk from there.

This walk takes you out of the old town through the Ploče gate, which is flanked by the stout Revelin fortress on the landward side, and by Fort St Luke (Sv. Luka) to seaward. The **suburb of Ploče** immediately outside the gate was, in former times, nothing more than a wide open space where the mule caravans would unload the produce they had brought in from the fertile Konavle valley to the east, and where Muslims from the Bosnian hinterland held a bazaar—on certain weekdays out of season, they still do. The old stone fountain that you see on your left has been there for at least a century and a half. Old postcards show it standing in splendid isolation, with one or two smallholdings behind it, and cultivated terraces piling steeply up the mountain behind, with mule tracks leading off into the wild interior. Now residential

Old postcard showing the Ploče area before it developed into a full-blown suburb.

housing scrambles up the hill. One of the suburbs is called Zlatni Potok ('Golden Stream'), supposedly because goods were traded for gold across a narrow creek which used to trickle down the hillside. Nowadays the creek is dry.

Below you to your right, near the water, is the site of the old town slaughterhouse. Beyond that is the lazaretto, the group of buildings that make up the **old quarantine hospital**. Plague first swept Dubrovnik in 1348, thought to have been spread by the Mongols as they skirmished their way across Europe. The outbreak lasted six months, during which an average of 120 people are reported to have died every day. Other outbreaks followed, and in 1377 Ragusa introduced quarantine requirements for ships, passengers and cargo. Originally the quarantine hospital was offshore, on the distant island of Sv. Andrija. Then it moved to Danče (*see pp. 145–6*), and finally to here. The last recorded outbreak of plague came in 1526, and the hapless merchant from Ancona who was suspected of bringing it was lynched by the furious citizens. The separate buildings of the quarantine hospital each have both road and sea access—look across each courtyard

and you will see the gates onto the water. Today they are used for folk dancing, parties and alternative arts events.

Continue up Frana Supila now. Just after the quarantine hospital is the **public beach of Banje**, with its restaurant and cocktail bar, a great favourite in the summer. Further on, you come to the **Hotel Excelsior**. The chapel of St Lazarus, patron saint of lepers and of the Knights Hospitallers, which used to serve the lazaretto (quarantine hospital), has now been incorporated into part of the hotel building. The hotel's Taverna Rustica restaurant is housed in an old

Taverna Rustica, once the home of Arthur Evans, now part of the Hotel Excelsior.

building once known as the Casa San Lazzaro. In 1882 it was home to Arthur Evans, who was working as a correspondent for the *Manchester Guardian*. His trips into Herzegovina displeased the Habsburg authorities, who arrested him as a suspected spy. Two years later Evans abandoned journalism for archaeology: he excavated Knossos, the palace of the mythical Minotaur, on Crete.

At the hotel Argentina the road divides. Take the lower road, which leads you past a turquoise-domed **Oriental folly**, now part of the Hotel Argentina and linked to it by a marble path across the lawn. Known locally as Sheherezade, this exuberant piece of self-indulgence was built at the beginning of the 20th century as a summer home for a Lithuanian banker. The architect was a Viennese, Alfred Keller. With its belvedere and Moorish pavilions on the sea and its terraced myrtle groves where a statue of Pan lurks, it is still an evocative place.

Next door to Sheherezade is a small chapel and gateway to the former Saraka family summer retreat, and still a private home. 'Keep away envy, disputes, ambition, cares,' reads the Latin inscription above the gate, 'caves, gardens and crags flourish here, in peace and tranquillity.' On the exterior wall of the chapel itself is a stone

Moorish pavilion at Sheherezade.

plaque telling you that the Ragusan mathematician **Marin Getaldić** (*see p. 84*) used a cave just below this site to conduct his numerous scientific experiments. The most famous of these involved using mirrors and magnifying glasses to set ships on fire, something that greatly perturbed the locals, who concluded that Getaldić was some kind of sorcerer. Presumably the ships had been forewarned of what lay in store.

A little way on from the chapel, you come to a treeless stretch, with an iron balustrade on the sea, and benches under the oleanders on the

other side of the road. Look out at Lokrum and you will clearly see, in a grove of tall cypresses by the water's edge, immediately under the ruins of Fort Royal, a solitary white cross. This marks the spot where the Austrian ship *Triton* exploded in 1859, with only a sole survivor—another example of the Lokrum curse (*see p. 150*).

Continue along the road for a little way, and you will come to a pair of green gates on your right, among a line of cypress trees. From here a path takes you down through a small park to the sea: local women gather here on summer evenings to fish for small fry from the rocks.

The road after this becomes quite narrow, with the wall on the right-hand side specially built to accommodate the trees. The road, **Vlaha Bukovca**, is named after Vlaho Bukovac, a local artist whose story is one of rags to respectability. Born Vlaho Fagioni (his father was of Italian extraction) in 1855, his early talent for drawing had to be forsaken for lack of money. Instead he went to the United States to make his fortune, before carving out a career in the merchant navy. He used his savings to put himself through the École des Beaux Arts in Paris, adopted the name Bukovac, and eventually went to England where he worked as a portrait painter. Portraits were to become the genre which made his name (*an example is reproduced on p. 169*).

Beyond the Hotel Villa Dubrovnik the road widens again, passing between elegant villas to right and to left, and taking you out to the **former monastery of St James** (Sv. Jakov Višnjica), a secluded spot where Ragusan emissaries were sent for a few days' quiet reflection, receiving and inwardly digesting their instructions before setting out on the perilous journey to the courts of temperamental Bans and Sultans and Grand Viziers, perpetually lustful for Ragusan silver. The Lithuanian banker owner of Sheherazade had plans to convert the monastery into a casino and to link Lokrum to the mainland by bridge. His grand schemes came to nothing though, and today the monastery belongs to the Croatian Academy of Sciences, though Sunday Mass is still held in the little church that adjoins it.

Behind the monastery a steep, zigzag flight of steps leads down to a lovely cove, with views back towards the old town. In summer the beach has a bar and café.

Steep descent down 163 steps to the beach of Sveti Jakov.

MUSIC IN RAGUSA

Who knows what plainsong echoed in the vaulted recesses of the Dominican and Franciscan churches, or what plangent lute music filled the night on summer evenings in patrician loggias. All those sounds are vanished on the desert air. Yet some echoes remain of Ragusa's musical past. Her most famous composer is Luka Sorkočević (1734–1789). The scion of a distinguished patrician family, Sorkočević travelled widely in Europe and, as Ragusa's ambassador to Vienna, struck up a friendship with Maria Theresa's court composer Gluck and—more importantly —with Joseph Haydn. Haydn was to have a profound influence on Sorkočević's compositional style: his piano sonatas are particularly fine, evoking a fragile world of graceful breeding, elegance and manners. In middle age Sorkočević suffered increasingly from depression. He committed suicide at the age of 55, throwing himself from the window of his town palace. His son Antun continued the family tradition of music and diplomacy. He was Ragusa's last ambassador to Paris before the Republic was dissolved by Napoleon. Recordings are available of both Sorkočevićs' work: try *Dubrovnik Gala* on the Musica Croatica label (published by Croatia Records).

The best Dalmatian folk music is *klapa*: sea shanties usually (but not exclusively) sung *a capella* by male voices. Most take the form of sentimental lyrics about the beloved homes and beloved mothers young sailors leave behind them when they take to the high seas. And for an easy-listening souvenir of your Dalmatian holiday, look no further than Oliver, the pure-gold crooner from Vela Luka on the island of Korčula. Recordings of all these and more are available from the CD shop on the Stradun, between Kunićeva and Nalješkovićeva (*map p. 198, C3*).

Lustful satyr and buxom maiden: fountain donated by the Amerling family in Brsalje's main square.

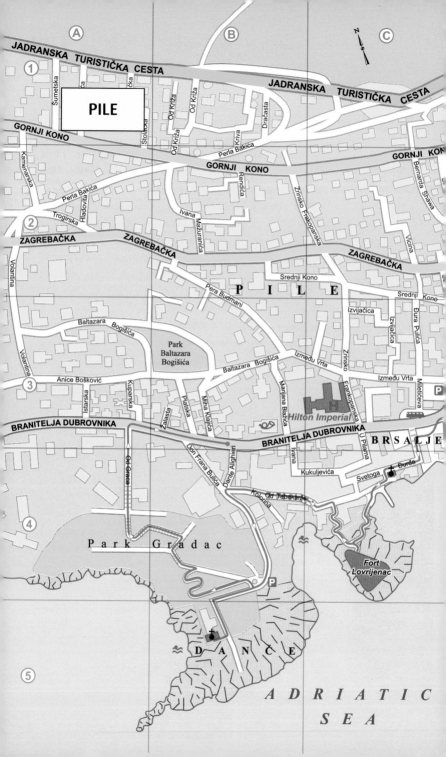

PILE & BRSALJE

The busy suburb of Pile, which links Dubrovnik old town to the port of Gruž, is also home to the city's first harbour, as well as a beautifully-situated little seaside nunnery. (NB: The loveliest thing on this walk is the nunnery church with its mediaeval paintings. Though it is sometimes open, it cannot be guaranteed. It is worth calling ahead to let them know you are coming. Tel: 414-098.)

This walk starts just outside the **Pile gate**. Look up at the gate and you will see, below the statue of St Blaise, a triple stone head. No one

knows for sure what it signifies, but in a town where legends abound that doesn't matter: there is always a story ready to supply the place of hard fact. In this case the story goes that the heads are portraits of two nuns and a monk, who developed a taste for illicit threesomes, and had their features replicated on the gate as a way of shaming them publicly.

Pile is and always has been a busy traffic terminus. At the beginning of the 20th century trams used to rattle up the hill to Gruž, but the gradient

The old rocky harbour of Brsalje lies just below Fort Bokar.

was too treacherous and the carriages were always careering off the rails, so the tracks were taken up and buses took the trams' place. Buses and taxis now crowd the square outside the gate, which is dominated on the right-hand side by the **old Pucić family summer residence**. The Pucić family had already moved out by the mid-19th century, when the building became the first place in Dubrovnik to offer accommodation to visitors, adopting the name Hotel Miramare. A little further up the hill is the Hilton Imperial, originally built in 1895 with money put up by a team of Austro-Hungarian doctors, who advocated sea bathing as the cure for all human ills.

Opposite the former Miramare, on the other side of the road, is a gravel park with a fountain in its centre (a gift to the town from the Amerling family) and a balustrade on the sea at the far end, with views out between Fort Bokar on the left and Lovrijenac on the right. In summer the Dubravka café puts tables out on the wide, sea-facing terrace.

At the roadside end of the park to your right, a short flight of steps leads you down into ulica Svetoga Đurđa. Go down these, and past the restored **chapel of St George**, always with an upturned boat or two outside it, and a single battered gravestone, carved with a trefoil cross. Beyond the chapel is a

small cove. This sleepy little inlet was once the city's harbour before what is now the old port and arsenal were constructed. It was also from here that the shallow creek that once followed the line of the Stradun snaked its way inland, rejoining the open sea at the site of the old port. In the 19th century this was a busy industrial centre, with a soap factory, weavers' workshops and wool dyers' yards. Today the harbour is used by locals as a base for small-fry fishing sprees. Looming above the cove is **Fort Lovrijenac**. To get to it, climb the steep steps to the left of the Orhan restaurant. Lovrijenac is open in the summer time: a ticket for the city walls gets you access. Above the entrance, look out for the famous inscription: *Non bene pro toto libertas venditur auro* ('Freedom should never be bartered for gold'). Lovrijenac was always regarded as the city's prime defensive structure. With seaward walls up to twelve metres thick, it was defended by a garrison under the command of a member of the nobility, who remained only for a single month before being replaced. Fears of potential treachery, it seems, ran high, because every month the garrison was supplied with exactly enough food to last it the four weeks: no opportunity was ever created for anyone to hole themselves up in the fortress and foment hostile, anti-Ragusan government feeling.

Fishing boat outside the chapel of St George in Brsalje.

Coming back from Lovrijenac, keep straight ahead down the other path, to come out on **Od Tabakarije**. The name has nothing to do with tobacco; it comes from the word for a tannery, which was another industry that took off in this area. Note the old stone flowerpots outside No. 14, directly opposite where you come out. These, known as *kamenice*, are not flowerpots at all, but were originally used for storing olive oil, sometimes with truckles of cheese floating in it. Cheese is still stored in oil today, but the receptacles are no longer made of stone. It is common to see large glass carboys of oil on restaurant counters, with great white cheeses submerged inside.

Turn left. The low stone lintel on the left, after house No. 41, is the entrance to a small, shingly beach where the local team practises water polo. Water polo is a popular sport in Dalmatia, and Dubrovnik is proud of its team's prowess. The inscription HAJDUK carved in the pavement just in front of a flight of steps a little further up Od Tabakarije was the handiwork of a fan of the Split football team.

Go on up the steps. At the top, to your left, is a fine large house with a horse's head adorning one of its doorways. Go straight on past the horse. Ahead of you is a tall building with slender palm trees outside it—the Dubrovnik Inter-University Center. Turn left before you reach it, up Don Frana Bulića, following the road up through a carpark, and then veering right to go down a cement-paved slope. Straight ahead of you, across the bay, you can see the burnt-out hulk of the former Hotel Libertas, destroyed in the 1991–92 war. Immediately below you on the left, through the cypress trees, you can see the pan-tiled roofs of the **Dance church and nunnery**. The church of Our Lady of Dance, and the pretty little Franciscan

The Franciscan convent of Danče, viewed from the sea.

convent that adjoins it, grew out of a small chapel first established here by public subscription in 1457, to serve the graveyard which stood nearby, the last resting place of paupers and felons, on a site which had once been a lepers' colony. Danče was also the site of Dubrovnik's first mainland quarantine station, before the one at Ploče was built (*see p. 136*). The little walled graveyard still exists, though it is not now tenanted by executed criminals. The church contains **two treasures of the Dubrovnik School**: a triptych by Božidarević (*see p. 97*). The high altar is a polyptych by Lovro Dobričević (*see p. 96*), which includes an image of St Julian the Hospitaller (bottom right, in the ermine-lined cloak), patron saint

of boatmen and wayfarers, often invoked as protector by hospitals and leper colonies, despite almost certainly being a mythical character and figment of the mediaeval imagination.

Beyond Danče church there is a place where you can swim from the rocks. If a ship passes out at sea, you might hear the church bell toll in greeting—a habit which the nuns have kept up for centuries. One of the bells was in fact donated by a sea captain.

Retrace your steps up to the carpark now, and turn left through the walls into **Gradac**, the 'Austrian park', so called because it was laid out in the 19th century, when Dubrovnik was part of the Habsburg empire. Today it is filled with fragments of statuary and would-be flowerbeds, and a goldfish pond with a fountain that still plays shyly and silently to itself, despite the fact that the halcyon days when top-hatted swells and wasp-waisted belles used the park as a trysting place have vanished.

Skirting left round the fountain, keep close to the left-hand boundary wall, and take the narrow path that runs alongside the brick-topped parapet. From here you have good views out toward the Lapad headland, once a slumbrous area of summer residences and cicada-song in the pine trees, but developed in the seventies and eighties into a resort centre for

mass tourism. Behind you and below you is the nunnery—you might see one of the nuns working diligently in the vegetable garden.

The path brings you up a flight of swithcback steps to join a broad gravel walk. Go left, and up more steps, turning right onto a platform with two benches, and then following the cobbled paths as it zig-zags up to the highest point. Go straight across another gravel walk, and through an old gateway to the steps of ulica Od Graca. Going down them you will have a fine old mansion—another Pucić family palace—to your right. It is now home to the Dubrovnik Symphony Orchestra. Od Graca brings you down into Branitelja Dubrovnika, the narrow, dusty, fume-filled **main thoroughfare of Pile**, lined with grand townhouses, but robbed by the incessant traffic of any air of gentility it may once have possessed. The disused chapel of the Visitation diagonally to your right looks grimy and forlorn. Turn right to go down the hill and back to the old town. About halfway back to the Pile gate, on your right, you will see Sesame, which serves good salads, either in its showbiz memorabilia-filled interior or on its pleasant raised summer terrace.

Interior of the nunnery church at Danče, with Dobričević's polyptych.

PART IV

DAY TRIPS

THE ISLANDS

p. 150 LOKRUM

p. 155 THE ELAPHITES

TRIPS ALONG THE DALMATIAN LITTORAL

p. 162 GRUŽ & RIJEKA DUBROVAČKA

p. 166 ZATON, TRSTENO & STON

p. 170 CAVTAT

The 'Dead Sea' on Lokrum.

LOKRUM

LOKRUM

NB: Boats to Lokrum leave regularly from Dubrovnik old port. Entrance tickets to the island must be purchased when you disembark. A map of the island and its sights is posted by the ticket desk.

On his way back from the Crusades, King Richard the Lionheart is said to have been shipwrecked on Lokrum and to have built a small chapel to give thanks that his life was spared. Nothing of that chapel survives. Little enough survives of the Benedictine monastery, which was established on the island in the 11th century, but dissolved under Napoleon. It was converted into a summer residence, in neo-Gothic style, by the Habsburg Archduke Maximilian, the younger brother of the Austrian emperor Franz Joseph, who used it—and the whole island—as a private summer residence, laying out ornamental gardens and glades of cypress and oleander. Local tongues wagged disapprovingly, calling what he had done to the old monastery an act of sacrilege and predicting dire consequences. Little did they know it, but their words were to turn prophetic. People soon began to talk of the Lokrum curse. In 1863 Maximilian was offered the title Emperor of Mexico by Napoleon III. In fact this was little more than a petty act of revenge on the part of France, who wanted to punish Mexico for defaulting on a loan. Franz Joseph was greatly troubled by the offer, knowing that his brother would be unwelcome in Mexico and possibly in danger. He urged Maximilian to refuse—but Maximilian had other ideas. Fatally he combined ambition for power and status with a dreamy, kindly disposition and a dislike of upsetting people—not a quality much called for in a political leader. He also had two forceful women at his back: his domineering mother, who thought that her darling Max deserved to be just as much an emperor as Franz Joseph; and his beautiful, socially ambitious wife, Charlotte of Belgium. As Franz Joseph had predicted, though, the appointment was a disaster. The Mexicans didn't care how affable Maximilian was; they didn't want him. In 1867 his disaffected subjects put an end to him and his regime by firing squad. His wife went raving mad and never recovered.

About ten years after the imperial tragedy Bishop Josip Strossmayer (*see p. 84*) put in a bid to buy Lokrum. Although born in Slavonia, Strossmayer loved

The red roofs of the former Benedictine monastery peep between Lokrum's celebrated green foliage. In the mid 19th century, the Habsburg Archduke Maximilian used Lokrum as a summer retreat, turning the monastery into his residence.

Dubrovnik and its environs, and found the landscape more congenial than that of his native home. His request was turned down, however, because Crown Prince Rudolf, Franz Joseph's son, wanted the island for himself. He spent part of his honeymoon here, and earth tremors were said to have been felt as the royal couple disembarked from their yacht. The Lokrum curse was preparing to do its worst. Eight years later, in 1889, Rudolf committed suicide at his hunting lodge near Vienna, having first shot dead his 17-year-old mistress. All that remains of the ruling house of Austria on Lokrum today is the Habsburg eagle carved in stone on the ruined house by the island's landing stage. And perhaps the peacocks that inhabit the island are the descendants of those that strutted in Maximilian's summer garden.

A restaurant and café now operates in the monastery ruins in the summer time. You can wander at leisure in the dilapidated cloister, with the remains of formal gardens on one side. Lokrum is also famed for its lush vegetation, and is a favourite haunt for young lovers. Apart from the monastery ruins, the island also boasts a botanic garden, with lines of agapanthus, and otherwise mainly cacti and palms. A sign pleads with people not to desecrate the larger cacti—in vain; some of the agave leaves are criss-crossed with initials and other graffiti, but this is a more time-honoured tradition than you might think. Entranced by the island's beauty and the scent of the jasmine on the night air, Archduke Maximilian himself is said to have carved a love heart pierced with his own and his wife's initials into the bark of one of Lokrum's oak trees.

Walking south from the monastery brings you to the 'Dead Sea' (*Mrtvo more*), a natural hollow filled with seawater, which seeps in through an underground channel. The water is shallow and warm, and a popular bathing place. If you prefer the open water, there are two good places to swim from the rocks: either in the sheltered channel facing Dubrovnik (just to your left as you arrive by boat), or on the seaward side, where the waves are rougher and the water colder, but where there are fewer people. Some of the rocks on this side were hollowed out into salt pans by the Benedictines—you can still see salt from the waves drying into a brittle white crust in them today. At the tip of the island furthest from the old town there is a nudist beach.

Walking north from the monastery, along the island's backbone, you will come to Fort Royal on its summit, a military redoubt and lookout point built by Marshal Auguste Frédéric Marmont when French troops occupied Ragusa in 1806.

Altar of the chapel of the Holy Cross on Lopud harbourfront.

THE ELAPHITES

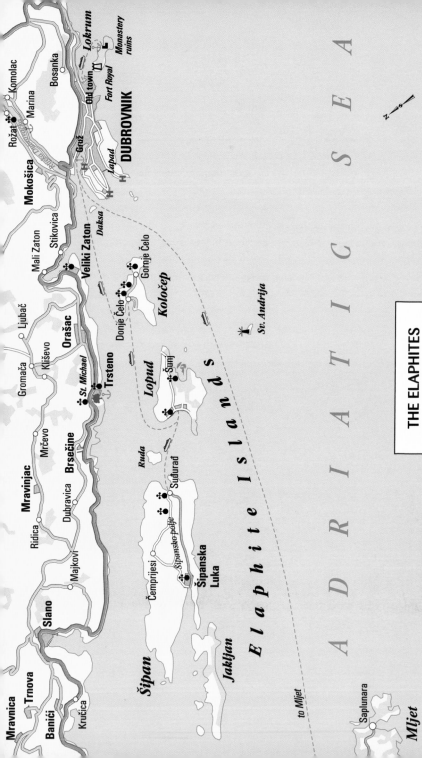

THE ELAPHITES

Komolac
Rožat
Marina
Bosanka
Mokošica
Gruž
Lapad
Old town
Fort Royal
Lokrum
Monastery ruins
DUBROVNIK

Mali Zaton
Stikovica
Veliki Zaton
Daksa
Gornje Čelo
Donje Čelo
Koločep
Sv. Andrija

Ljubač
Orašac
Kliševo
Gromača
Mrčevo
Trsteno
St. Michael
Lopud
Šunj

Dubravica
Ridica
Brsečine
Ruda
Sudurad

Mravinjac
Majkovi
Čemprijesi
Šipanska Luka
Šipansko polje

Mravnica
Trnova
Banići
Slano
Kručica
Šipan
Jakljan

Elaphite Islands

ADRIATIC SEA

to Mljet
Saplunara
Mljet

N

THE ELAPHITES

NB: Boats to the Elaphites leave from the port of Gruž. Timetables are available from the Jadrolinija office at Stjepana Radića 40 (the main street) in Gruž, or from the information office on the Stradun, next to the Festival café.

The islands that make up the Elaphite archipelago number thirteen in all, of which the main three are described below. Despite their lack of natural fresh water springs (though there is water flowing in the limestone underground), the islands have always been inhabited, first by Illyrian tribes, then by Greeks, then by the Romans, and finally by the Slavs, who arrived in the 7th century. The islands came into the possession of Ragusa in early mediaeval times and remained there until the fall of the Ragusan Republic, with the major islands having their own rector, and attracting their share of summer residences for the nobility. Today their permanent population stands at around 1,000.

A Jadrolinija ferry plying its familiar way between the major Elaphite Islands.

KOLOČEP

This is the smallest of the three major Elaphites, once famous for its coral divers, who worked the beds around the island of Sv. Andrija, the most distant of all the islands: tiny, uninhabited and dominated by its lighthouse. By the 16th century the reefs had been completely stripped, and the divers migrated further afield to find work. The two main settlements on Koločep are Gornje Čelo to the south-east and Donje Čelo to the north-west. A very pretty walled lane links the two, taking you past vegetable and fruit gardens and a number of ancient chapels, some of which still preserve fragments of ancient Croatian braided stonework (*see p. 87*). Donje Čelo, the larger of the two villages, has the better choice of cafés and places to eat.

LOPUD

The second largest of the Elaphites, Lopud has less evidence of agricultural activity than Koločep, perhaps because it is better adapted for making its living out of tourism, and perhaps also because of a strong maritime history: Ragusan Admirals of the Fleet were traditionally from Lopud. Lopud has only a single settlement, which stretches out along the main harbour, from the picturesque Franciscan monastery and church of St Mary at one end to the rather less picturesque Hotel Lafodia at the other. The church and monastery are not always open, but if you can get in, the church has a number of interesting paintings in it (notably an *Our Lady with Flowers* by a painter of the Flemish school) and beautiful 15th-century choir stalls. The empty, disused monastery, with its old gardens stretching down to the sea, is well worth an atmospheric wander.

Sadly Lopud's existence has been too turbulent for much to have remained intact over the years. Its position has made it an important strategic site for military and naval conflict, notably during the Napoleonic Wars. Blockading the French, the British captured the Elaphites and issued a proclamation from Lopud to the effect that 'the English and Austrian forces are advancing towards this country to give it back its liberty'. The Austrians didn't quite see it that way. Though the British had happily saluted the Ragusan flag, the Austrians were swift to hoist their own standard from Orlando's column in Dubrovnik old town. When the British fleet left the area in 1814, leaving the Austrians in

Lopud harbour, with the Franciscan church tower in the background.

charge, the nobles who thought that their beloved Republic had been restored, learned instead that they were the subjects of Emperor Franz I, instructed to 'try to deserve the effects of his benevolence by a prompt and loyal submission'. Perfidious Albion had left them in the lurch. A sad and inglorious end to so many centuries of independence.

Above Lopud harbour, just as you alight from the boat, you can still see what remains of the island's Rector's palace (very little, but there is a three-light Gothic window frame still standing). Reportedly this was once a stunning example of the Gothic-Renaissance transitional style, the style which is so characteristic of Ragusa's golden age.

Lopud's most famous son is Miho Pracat, the wealthy shipowner who left his entire fortune to the Ragusan Republic when he died, and who is honoured with a bust in the atrium of the Rector's Palace—the only such monument ever erected to a commoner. Pracat was born on Lopud in around 1522. His success did not come easily or instantly. According to a popular legend, his enterprises failed twice, and he twice lost his entire fleet and his fortune. Sitting gloomily on a wall on his native island, he wiled away the time watching the antics of a

The beautiful sandy bay of Šunj.

lizard as it tried to climb upwards. Twice it fell and had to start again. The third time it succeeded. Instantly reading a moral lesson into this, Pracat resolved to try and seek his fortune one more time. He succeeded. Pracat's house used to stand on the waterfront. It is no longer there, but the chapel he endowed survives, the chapel of the Holy Cross (*pictured on p. 153*), set a little way back from the street. The ruined building next door, used now as a haybarn, may perhaps have been Pracat's house. A few paces closer to the Franciscan monastery is another pretty chapel, tucked into a tiny alley, and dedicated to St Jerome, the Dalmatian scholar-hermit who produced the Vulgate Bible.

Lopud harbour offers a number of places to eat and drink. For swimming, the best beach is Šunj, on the other side of the island, accessible by a winding track. Šunj is one of those wonderful beaches where the sandbank stretches a long way out, making the shallow water beautifully warm, and meaning that it takes quite a time before you get out of your depth. Above the beach stands the chapel of Our Lady of Šunj, built, according to the legend, by a member of the Visconti family, whose prayers to the Virgin had saved him from shipwreck against the Lopud cliffs. The Visconti family coat of arms, which shows a snake devouring a child, is the same as the coat of arms of Lopud. The chapel of Our Lady of Šunj contains a very fine altarpiece with a carved wooden sculpture of the Virgin and twelve apostles. It is said that Miho Pracat found the figures in London on one of his travels, and learning that the English had no use for them—Catholic shrines to the Virgin being out of vogue while the Reformation raged—he brought them back to Lopud. The story is possibly untrue. The saucer-shaped halos worn by the twelve apostles look extremely Ragusan.

ŠIPAN

The largest of the Elaphites and the most fertile, with its main port of Šipanska Luka linked to the little fishing port of Suđurađ by the fertile valley of Šipansko polje, Šipan is noted for its connection with two great men. One of these is Lodovico Beccadelli, a Catholic Cardinal and friend of Michelangelo, who came from Rome at Dubrovnik's request to act as Bishop of Dubrovnik and to help

The pretty little fishing port of Suđurađ on the island of Šipan, home to the 16th-century summer residence of the seafaring, merchant-trading Skočibuha family.

strengthen the Republic's ties to the mother church. Writing about him in a letter to a friend, Michelangelo expressed sympathy for the hard life Beccadelli was consigned to, with only the barren ocean in front of him and the barren mountains behind, filled with wild tribes. In view of Dubrovnik's subsequent history, it is tempting to conclude that not a great deal has changed. A plaque to Beccadelli's memory is fixed to the wall of the old Archbishop's summer residence in Šipansko polje.

The small, scruffy, pretty fishing port of Suđurađ contains the turreted, fortress-like summer residence of Tomo Skočibuha and his son Vice, a man who was to become one of the wealthiest mariners and merchants of the Republic and who, though not a patrician himself, was able to live in patrician style. His town palace in Dubrovnik (*see pp. 114–15*) is the finest Renaissance secular building that remains in the old town today. Skočibuha is also reported to have been a great patron of the arts—in fact a portrait of him exists, shown playing the part of donor in Santi di Tito's *Descent of the Holy Spirit*, in the collection of the Dominican friary. Sadly this is not on public display, but a copy of the portrait can be found in the Maritime Museum. For his services to the Republic Skočibuha was offered a noble title, but he lost interest when informed that it would not be hereditary. He died in 1588, with any luck before news of Dubrovnik's disastrous involvement in the Spanish Armada broke— news which would have chilled the cockles of any patriotic naval man—and is buried in the Dominican church.

The Franciscan monastery of Rožat on the Rijeka Dubrovačka. The whole river valley, half salt water half fresh, was a favourite summer retreat for the old Ragusan aristocracy.

GRUŽ & RIJEKA
DUBROVAČKA

GRUŽ &
RIJEKA DUBROVAČKA

NB: To find the places mentioned in this section, see the map of the Dalmatian coast on p. 154.

The trip takes you first through **Gruž**, the main harbour of Dubrovnik, and a busy, bustling place best known for its Friday fishmarket. When a boat comes in with a really large fish, which no one person can afford to buy, the local shoppers set up a sort of lottery system: everyone pays ten kuna, and then lots are drawn to see who wins the fish.

After the earthquake of 1667, concerned voices urged the Ragusan government to consider relocating the whole city to Gruž—a less seismic zone, with a deeper harbour. These calls were ignored. Had they been heeded, Dubrovnik might have prospered better in the 19th century, but it would

have been a lot less beautiful today. Gruž is a traffic-choked, workaday part of town, though the views across the harbour, with the little yachts at anchor and the graceful Sorkočević summer palace on the further bank are pretty enough. Opposite the main Port of Dubrovnik harbour building rises the tall campanile of the church with a Dominican cloister attached. Remains of boathouses still survive on this side, their arcades now used as shops and bars.

Where the River Ombla (Dubrovačka) gushes above ground in Komolac.

Old postcard showing the Rijeka Dubrovačka, dominated by the high ridge that separates Croatia from Montenegro. The former Sorkočević summer palace stands in the grove of tall cypresses in the centre of the picture.

Beyond Gruž and its large Konzum store are the tall harp-strings of the road bridge across the Rijeka. This bridge takes the bulk of the traffic and leaves the **Rijeka Dubrovačka** inlet to the right relatively quiet. The valley here was created by an earthquake and is fed by the sea at one end and by a river at the other, making the water a mixture of fresh and salt. At one time it was a favourite summer resort for the Ragusan nobility, and as you drive up the right-hand bank today, you pass a number of ruinous summer residences, some of which have their own private chapel attached, as was the custom. Sadly none of these great empty hulks is open to the public, but at Komolac, the village at the head of the inlet, the former Sorkočević (Sorgo) residence has been incorporated into the Miho Pracat yachting marina, and you can wander freely around its grounds. Fronted by what remains of French-style formal gardens and specially constructed private fishponds, the palace has its own landing stage, where the family would have disembarked with bag and baggage for the summer, entering the house via the wide stone steps adorned with carved stone baskets of fruit.

The view from here across the clear, turquoise-green water to the Franciscan monastery at Rožat is one of the best that the Rijeka affords, giving something of an idea of how idyllically tranquil life must have been in those 16th-century salad days. The remains of agricultural terracing climbs high up the steep mountainside opposite—the larders of the patrician palaces would not have lain empty. Nor would their inmates have suffered from the summer heat. The river that fills the inlet from inland, the Dubrovačka (Ombla), runs underground through limestone caverns for much of its length, but here at Komolac it emerges, gushing to the surface in an ice-cold glassy torrent, cooling the air that surrounds it as well as the water that comes in from the sea.

The mournful, derelict state of the old summer palaces today is not entirely due to 20th-century conflicts and depredations. When Napoleon's men occupied Dubrovnik in 1806, the Russians mounted a siege on the city, hoping to capture it for themselves. They were assisted by bands of unruly Montenegrin bandits, who poured down from their mountain fastnesses and, unable to believe their eyes at the wealth and riches contained in the summer mansions of Rijeka Dubrovačka, duly sacked and looted them all.

When you have rounded the tip of the inlet and crossed the Ombla, instead of following the main road, turn left down the narrow lower road, which hugs the bank and takes you past the old monastery—a gentler and more picturesque route.

Neptune's grotto, an 18th-century folly in the Gučetić arboretum at Trsteno.

ZATON, TRSTENO & STON

ZATON, TRSTENO
& STON

NB: Zaton and Trsteno are marked on the map on p. 154. Ston is shown on the Dalmatian littoral map on p. 6.

The settlement of **Zaton** is divided into two, Veliki and Mali, straddling the bay ('*zaton*' in Croatian) which gives the villages their name. Fishing boats and small yachts tie up at Veliki Zaton, which boasts a couple of waterfront restaurants, notably the Ankora. Across the water is the Orsan, which has been run for decades by the Gverović family, and is built into the former boathouse ('*orsan*') of a patrician summer residence. It was here that the Renaissance poetess and famed Ragusan beauty Cvijeta Zuzorić held summer salons, and had minstrels and wordsmiths such as Torquato Tasso swooning at her dainty feet.

View across the water to the Ankora restaurant at Veliki Zaton.

The Gučetić summer residence at Trsteno.

Trsteno is a tiny hamlet, but worth a visit for its beautiful arboretum and Gučetić (Gozze) family summer residence. A member of the family is said to have planted an oak tree before setting out on the Last Crusade. Great things grow from little acorns. The ornamental park that now surrounds the summer villa is a beautiful place for a summer or springtime stroll, and is notable for its early 18th-century folly, Neptune's grotto, where Neptune stands flanked by tritons and dolphins, all merrily spitting water in graceful arcs into the fishpond at their feet. During Ragusa's heyday Gučetić gathered poets and men of culture about him, one of whom was Titian, who is said to have painted the altarpiece in the chapel of St Michael in Trsteno village (*see box on following page*). When Gučetić had political matters to attend to, he and other members of the Great Council would congregate at Trsteno, around an outdoor meeting table. The great and mighty pronouncements made by the gathering were noted down by a scribe whose desk was especially fashioned so as not to face the meeting, to allow the voice of government to maintain its anonymity. The table still exists, as does the scribe's desk. Walking back to the house from the Neptune fountain, turn right into a little mossy glade, and you will find it there, waiting for the master's return. The house and garden remained in the Gučetić family until 1947, when they were confiscated by the state. Byron is said to have been a visitor here. A less welcome guest was the Napoleonic marshal, Auguste Frédéric Marmont, who stayed here in 1806–8, in the front-facing upstairs room with the coffered ceiling. Marmont, who loved an aristocratic title as much as his master Bonaparte, was thrilled when Napoleon created him Duc de Raguse in 1808.

The combined settlements of **Veliki and Mali Ston** formerly constituted the second largest town in the Ragusan Republic, a town that Napoleon was more eager to acquire than Dubrovnik itself, not only because of its strategic position at the head of the Pelješac peninsula, but also because of its valuable salt works. Today Ston is more famous for its great fortifying walls—proudly announcing themselves to be second in length only to the Great Wall of China—which stretch from Mali Ston on one side over the hill to Veliki Ston on the other. Standing on the ramparts at Veliki Ston, you get an excellent view of the salt pans, still in use today, as well as of the town itself. Mali Ston's great claim to fame are its oysters. In 1939 at a food fair in London they were voted the finest in the world. Today you can sample them at one of Mali Ston's waterfront restaurants, from where you also have a view of the wooden trestles in the water on which they are farmed. Needless to say, the best months to visit Ston are those which have an R in them.

THE CHAPEL OF ST MICHAEL AT TRSTENO

Titian was once a guest at the Gučetić summer home, and as a token of thanks he is said to have painted an altarpiece for the village chapel of St Michael, using his host's son as the model for the Archangel's face. You can see the chapel up in the hills a little way beyond the arboretum to the north, surrounded by a cluster of cypresses. To get to it, follow the main road through the village, taking a fork to the right, up a minor road that leads gently uphill. The chapel is on your left. Though always locked, the key is kept locally, and it is worth asking at the houses across the road if anyone can let you in. Donations to church upkeep will be appreciated. The attribution of the painting to Titian has never been formally accepted; experts are more inclined to believe that it is the work of Titian's studio. The subject deserves investigation—but whatever the truth, let us hope that the altarpiece will remain *in situ* here for many centuries to come.

Portrait by Vlaho Bukovac (1855–1922), Cavtat's most famous son.

CAVTAT

CAVTAT

NB: Boats to Cavtat leave regularly from Dubrovnik old harbour. The journey—seven nautical miles—takes about 40–45 minutes, depending on weather conditions. Cavtat is marked on the map on p. 6.

I n the little church of Our Lady of the Snows, at the western end of the main harbour, there is a frieze above the chancel arch by the local-born artist Vlaho Bukovac (*see opposite*) depicting Cavtat harbour. Though the scene is not quite as tranquil and picturesque today as it was in the artist's romantic 19th-century imagination, it is pretty nearly so. Flanked by stone houses, built at the same time as those in Dubrovnik's Stradun and looking remarkably similar, fringed by palm trees and pavement cafés, and with a slender church steeple at either end, Cavtat's horseshoe-shaped main harbour is very pretty indeed, and genuinely unspoiled.

Cavtat, formerly known as Ragusa Vecchia, began life as the classical city of Epidaurum. Originally a Greek settlement, it was Romanised by the Emperor

View of the palm-fringed Cavtat harbour.

Augustus in the 1st century BC, and is said to have been the birthplace of Aesculapius, god of medicine, the son of Apollo's encounter with a sea nymph. It was from here, when the city was sacked and burned by the barbarian Avars in the 7th century, that the founders of today's Ragusa are thought to have set sail, to establish their city afresh on an unhospitable rocky outcrop some 17 kilometres up the coast.

The church of Our Lady of the Snows, which is attached to the Franciscan monastery, also contains an exquisite mediaeval altarpiece of St Michael (1510), the only-known surviving work of Vicko Lovrin, son of Lovro Dobričević (*see p. 96*). Ruins of Cavtat's ancient amphitheatre have been unearthed near the church; still more lies under the sea. From the church you can walk right round the headland to the next bay, under which Epidaurum lies buried until the crack of doom, along with a couple of ancient shipwrecks further out. The tourist office in the town can give you details of diving trips to see the ruins, which are organised in the summer.

At the top of the hill above Our Lady of the Snows, in a grove of pine and cypress, is the town cemetery, dominated by the bright white mausoleum of the wealthy, shipowning Račić family (*see p. 32*). On the way up the hill you will pass a doorway with a Latin inscription above it which reads: 'I have little; I am content with little; a little is enough for me'. Not a sentiment that would have found much sympathy in Račić circles. Their magnificent mausoleum, beautifully set on top of its hill, looking out to sea, is obscurely Christiano-Babylonian in its overall effect, with a frieze of winged sheep and rams' heads running all the way around the top. Its entranceway is flanked by two slender caryatids, half angel-half high priestess. The bronze main door is decorated with the signs of the zodiac as well as with stylised images of the four apostles of the Slavs: Sava, Gregory, Cyril and Methodius. It was Cyril and Methodius who invented Glagolitic, the old Slavonic script which eventually mutated into the alphabet now known as Cyrillic, and which is used here for the raised inscriptions on the mausoleum door. Built in the early 1920s, the mausoleum is the work of the Croatian sculptor Ivan Meštrović (*see p. 99*).

The former house and atelier of Vlaho Bukovac is open to the public on ulica Bukovčeva. Born into a poor family in 1855, Bukovac spent his early life outside Croatia, seeking his fortune as a sailor. It was thanks to the patronage of two influential men, one of them Bishop Strossmayer (*see p. 84*), that Bukovac turned to painting, his natural inclination, becoming the first Croatian to be elected a member of the Paris Salon. Though his dearest wish in old age was to spend his last years in Cavtat, he died in Prague in 1922.

PART V

PRACTICALITIES

p. 173 FOOD & WINE
Wine - p. 174

p. 175 RESTAURANTS
Restaurant locator map - p. 178
Cafés - p. 180

p. 183 HOTELS & ACCOMMODATION

p. 186 PRACTICAL TIPS

PRACTICALITIES

FOOD & WINE

The cuisine of Dalmatia is simple and good, relying on the quality of the local ingredients rather than on elaborate sauces or disguising spice. Fish predominates, supplemented by cured ham, a few cheeses, and Italian-influenced risottos and pasta dishes, including black risotto, which is made with squid ink. Fresh salads are plentiful in the spring and summer season, supplemented at colder times of year by shredded white and purple cabbage, lightly pickled, and usually quite delicious. Cheeses range from tangy and crumbly sheep's cheese to very young, fresh curd, often mixed with cream and spread on slices of corn bread as an *amuse-gueule*. The most common cooked vegetable you will be offered is *blitva* (Swiss chard), which can be deliciously

The beautifully situated terrace of the Orhan restaurant in the oldest part of Pile, with views over Fort Bokar and the city walls.

done with garlic, olive oil and a touch of lemon juice, or cruelly boiled to death in barely salted water.

With fish, the preparation methods are very simple—grilled or fried—and again the cooking relies on the quality of the raw ingredients rather than the sleight of hand of the chef. It's worth asking to see what they've got, and as far as possible satisfying yourself that it really is fresh, rather than recently thawed. Desserts do not play a major role in Dalmatian cooking. One pudding with a claim to native speciality status is *rozata*, similar to creme caramel.

WINE

Most restaurants serve wine both loose, by the glass or carafe, and bottled. The loose wine can be excellent, but it can also be rather oxidised if you are unlucky enough to get the tail end of a container that has been open for a while. This is more of a problem with the red wine than with the white, which can respond to oxidation rather well, developing a lovely deep golden colour and a slight sherry-like bite.

Most of the best local wine comes from the Pelješac peninsula or from Korčula. Good, fruity dry whites include Pošip and Grk. The Plavac Mali is the famous red grape of the region, thought to be genetically similar to California's Zinfandel. In fact it was a Croatian emigré winemaker, Miljanko Grgić, who first made the world sit up and notice Californian wine when French wine tasters at a comparative tasting in 1976 scored his wines higher than their own Bordeaux. Grgić now operates both in California and at home on Pelješac. The best red wine of all is meant to come from the Dingač area.

Prošek is a sweet wine, tawny red in colour, usually drunk well chilled with a cube or two of ice in the glass. Travarica is a strong grappa flavoured with herbs. Pelinkovac is a bitter liqueur distilled from aromatic plants.

RESTAURANTS

The following list is entirely subjective, being a personal selection of favourite restaurants. It makes no attempt to be exhaustive—there are plenty of good restaurants which are not included. The numbers cross-refer to the map on p. 178.

1 ANTUNINI *Map p. 178, C2*
Interesting for its interior decor—a recreation of a wealthy merchant's living room—which makes it a good choice for a cool or rainy evening. The fish stew is pricey but very tasty. *Prijeko 30. Tel: 321-199. 9am–1am.*

2 DUNDO MAROJE *Map p. 179, D3*
One of the few restaurants in the old town that stays open year-round, attracting a faithful following of local diners. Traditional Ragusan fare, all served from a tiny, hole-in-the-wall kitchen next door to the restaurant. In summer there is a terrace tucked inside the street, on the Stradun corner. *Kovačka 1.*

3 EAST WEST Map p. 134, B
African rugs, Indian cushions and Cuban music come together in a fusion confusion against an Adriatic backdrop on Banje beach. The menu includes pasta dishes, burgers and

Interior of the Antunini restaurant on Prijeko, named after old Ragusa's premier guild of merchants, and decorated to look like a wealthy bourgeois salon.

club sandwiches as well as more traditional dishes such as black risotto or lamb *ražnjići* (small pieces on a skewer). The marinated fish (steaks of *lokarda*, similar to swordfish) is excellent. *Banje Beach Club, Frana Supila b.b. Tel: 412-220.*

4 KAMENICE *Map p. 179, D4*
The market traders have a bite to eat here before they set up their stalls for

the day. Busy at lunchtime, with a mixture of locals and tourists. Good, simple menu and reasonable prices, though service can be a bit brusque. The risotto with mussels and a mixed salad makes a very good lunch. *Gundulićeva poljana b.b.*

⑤ LOKANDA PESKARIJA *Map p. 179, E4*
Bustling, friendly bar and restaurant right on the old port, adjoining the fish market. Delicious fresh fish and good salads. Simple, cleanly made local wine by the glass. NB: This place is very popular with locals too; in high season you may have to wait for a table. *Na Ponti b.b. Tel: 324-750. 8am–midnight.*

⑥ MEA CULPA *Map p. 178, B3*
Locally known as the best pizzeria in town, because it has a real wood-fired pizza oven—though when business is brisk, they do tend to use the electric oven too. Pasta dishes also on offer, and salad as a side order. *Za Rokom 3. Tel: 424-819. 8am–midnight.*

⑦ NAUTIKA *Map p. 178, A2*
Just outside the Pile gate, this is Dubrovnik's premier restaurant, and a cut above the rest in terms of service, presentation, cooking—and price.

Lokanda Peskarija in the old port, one of the best places to eat in the old town.

Good salads and risottos. Either eat inside, or on the raised outdoor terrace overlooking the sea. *Brsalje 3. Tel: 442-526. Noon–midnight.*

8 PENATUR *Map p. 179, D3*
Simple, unpretentious menu of pasta (the tortellini is the best), fish dishes or steaks. Serves cheap meals at lunchtimes, and reasonable à la carte in the evenings, in a small, cosy setting. Tables outside abutting the church of St Blaise in summer. *Lučarica 2.*

9 POSAT *Map p. 178, B2*
Very pretty raised outdoor terrace just outside the Pile gate. Popular with locals, who swear by the cuisine. Traditional menu, predominantly of seafood. *Uz Posat 1. Tel: 421-194. 11am–midnight.*

10 PROTO *Map p. 178, C3*
A *proto*, in Ragusan, is a master shipbuilder. On this restaurant's outdoor upper terrace, you sit surrounded by swifts wheeling and scrambling into nests in the surrounding walls. Mussels in thick oil and garlic sauce and vegetables Župa Dubrovačka style (potatoes with rosemary) are particularly good. Winter garden and downstairs dining room for inclement weather. Shares ownership with Nautika. *Široka 1. Tel: 323-234. 11am–11pm.*

East West down on Banje beach, a stylish enclave beside the deep blue Adriatic.

11 ROZARIJ *Map p. 179, D2*
Tucked into a corner behind the church of Sv. Nikola, this is a very pretty spot for dinner. Friendly service, honest food. *Prijeko 2. Tel: 321-257. 11am–midnight.*

12 SPAGHETTERIA TONI *Map p. 178, C4*
Locals will tell you that Toni serves the best pasta in town. There is certainly a wide choice, and good salads to go with it. No espressos or cappuccinos here, only Turkish coffee. *Božidarevića 14. Tel: 323-134.*

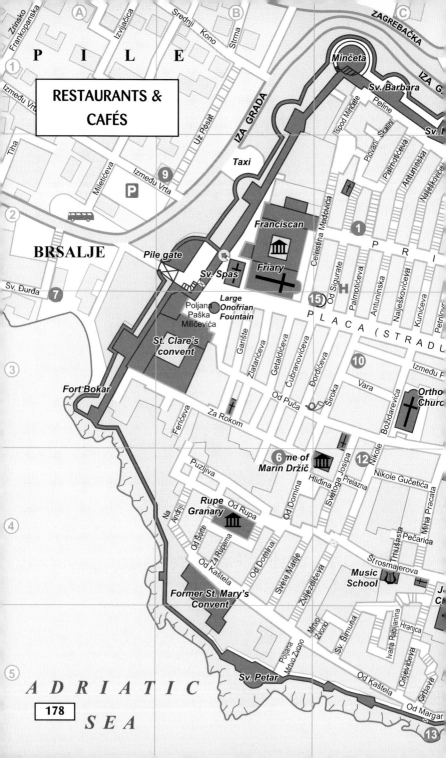

RESTAURANTS & CAFÉS

PILE

BRSALJE

M*inčeta*

Sv. Barbara

Taxi

Franciscan

Friary

Pile gate

Sv. Spas

Large Onofrian Fountain

Poljana Paška Miličevića

St. Clare's convent

Fort Bokar

PLACA (STRADU

Ortho Churc

me of Marin Držič

Rupe Granary

Music School

Former St. Mary's Convent

Sv. Petar

A D R I A T I C

178

S E A

Sv. Đurđa

Za Rokom

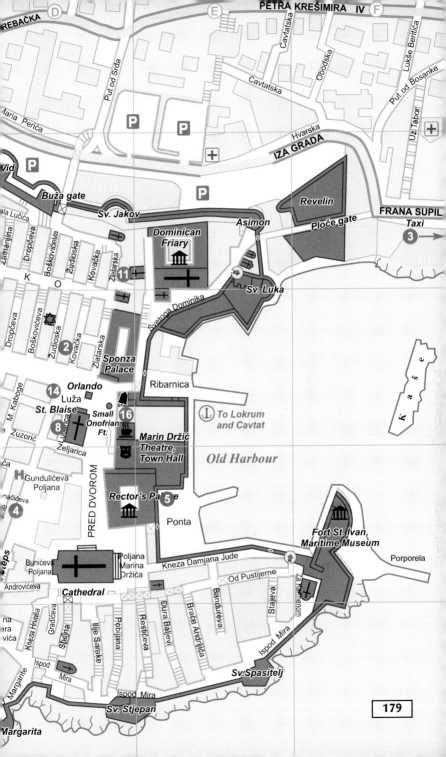

REBAČKA

PETRA KREŠIMIRA IV

D   E   F

Cavtatska

Obodska

Lukše Bertića

Put od Bosanke

Maria Perića

Put od Srđa

Cavtatska

Uz Tabor

P   P

Hvarska

IZA GRADA

P

Vid   P

Buža gate

FRANA SUPIL

la Lučića

Sv. Jakov

Asimon

Revelin

Ploče gate

Taxi

3

Zelanjina

Dropčeva

Boškovićeva

Žudioska

Kovačka

Zlatarska

Dominican
Friary

11

Sv. Luka

Dropčeva

Boškovićeva

Žudioska

Kovačka

Zlatarska

2

Svetoga Dominika

Sponza
Palace

Ribarnica

Orlando

14

Luža

St. Blaise

8

Zuzorić

Zeljarica

Small
Onofrian
Ft.

16

Marin Držić
Theatre,
Town Hall

To Lokrum
and Cavtat

Old Harbour

M. Kaboge

H   Gundulićeva
Poljana

4   načićeva

PRED DVOROM

Rector's Palace

5

Ponta

Fort St. Ivan,
Maritime Museum

Porporela

teps

Bunićeva
Poljana

Poljana
Marina
Držića

Kneza Damjana Jude

Androvićeva

Cathedral

Od Pustijerne

na
era
vića

Kneza Hvara

Gradićeva

Stulina

Ilije Sarake

Pobijana

Restićeva

Đura Baljevi

Braće Andrijića

Bandureva

Stajeva

Ispod Mira

Za Kamenom

Ispod

Margarita

Mira

Ispod Mira

Sv.Spasitelj

Sv. Stjepan

Margarita

K
a
š
e

179

CAFÉS

Although many people drink Turkish coffee at home, when they go out, their habits become Italian. Espresso and cappuccino are much more readily available, and that is what almost all the cafés serve. Many—but not all—of Dubrovnik's best cafés are on the Stradun. Below are some favourites. Numbers refer to the map on p. 178.

13 BUŽA *Map p. 178, C5*
Small, palm-shaded waterfront bar perched on a ledge outside the city walls. Access is a twisting descent down stone steps from a gate in the walls themselves. Coffee, travarica, cool beer, lemonade and ice creams available. *Between the bastions of Sv. Petar and Sv. Margarita. Access from Od* *Margarite. Follow the sign that says 'Cold Drinks'.*

14 CAFÉ CELE *Map p. 179, D3*
Middle-aged locals love this place, which is what gives it its character. It is best for an early evening drink, after the sun has sunk and the light is beginning to fade, and when the pigeons come

The Festival Café on the Stradun, one of the best-looking cafés in Dubrovnik in terms of indoor and outdoor furnishings, and serving the city's best cakes.

home to their night-time perches on the church of St Blaise. Cele also has the distinction of being the only café in Dubrovnik to show any trace of former Austro-Hungarian influence. The pastry selection here is reminiscent of Vienna or Budapest. *Stradun 1.*

15 FESTIVAL *Map p. 178, B3*
Housed in a building that was gutted by fire in the 1991–92 war, this place proves that phoenixes really can rise from their ashes. The Festival is unquestionably the best-looking café in town, with the best sticky cakes and glorious Spanish-style hot chocolate that you can practically stand the spoon up in. They also do the best café breakfast in town: toast, butter, jam and orange juice. *Stradun b.b.*

View of the terrace of the Gradska Kavana, looking towards the cathedral.

16 GRADSKA KAVANA *Map p. 179, D3*
It doesn't serve the best coffee or the best cakes, but it attracts a faithful following of regulars whose faces you will begin to recognise, and its elevated terrace is a perfect vantage point for watching the world go by. A very pleasant spot to sit out in the evening with a glass of iced *prošek.* *Pred Dvorom 3.*

Enjoying a quiet Ožujsko with a view of the limitless horizon at Buža.

FOOD FOR PICNICS

Below is a selection of the easiest places to buy ingredients for a picnic.

MARKETS

The street market on Gundulićeva poljana (*map p. 199, D4*) is a good place for fruit, salad ingredients and fresh cheese. (*Open until 1pm weekdays, and all day Sat.*) The larger produce market at Gruž is on the right-hand side of the main waterfront street.

SUPERMARKETS

There are small Konzum stores just outside the Pile and Ploče gates (Branitelja Dubrovnika and Frana Supila respectively). There are also two general shops selling wine, water and groceries on Od Puča (Nos. 8 and 12; *map pp. 199, D4–198 C3*).

BREAD & SANDWICHES

The sandwich bar at Lučarica 2 (*map p. 199, D3*) sells ready-made sandwiches, as does the bakery at Od Puča 11 (*map p. 198, C3*). Pita bread and filled burek are sold at Zlatni Puder, on the corner of Peline and Boškovićeva (*map p. 198, D2*). Tanti Gusti on Između polača 11 and the bakery at Od Puča 11 (*both map p. 198, C3*) both have a good selection of bread, cakes and pastries.

HOTELS & ACCOMMODATION

Postal addresses are Dubrovnik, postcode 20000. Telephone numbers are Dubrovnik, code 020 from inside Croatia or +385 20 from abroad. Prices vary considerably, and are generally cheaper through travel agents. This is an approximate guide for high season prices, for a double room per night, excluding taxes.

GRAND VILLA ARGENTINA, VILLA ORSULA & SHEHEREZADE *Map p. 134, C*
Frana Supila 14
Tel: 440-555
www.gva.hr
159 rooms, 7 suites. € 230–390
An old and a new building fused together and sumptuously decorated to give a grand, international hotel feel. The older wing (built in 1922) once boasted Burton and Taylor, von Karajan and Callas as guests. Good location, a short walk from the Ploče gate, and built right on the waterfront, with private beach and swimming. The Villa Orsula next door is an elegant 1936 seafront villa. On the other side is the turquoise-domed Sheherezade (renovation almost complete at the time of writing).

EXCELSIOR *Map p. 134, B*
Frana Supila 12
Tel: 353-353
www.hotel-excelsior.hr
170 rooms. € 138–230
High-specification hotel, recently fully renovated. Located on the sea very close to the old town, in the Ploče district. The focus seems to be on business use, with fully up-to-date conference facilities.

HILTON IMPERIAL *Map p. 142, C3*
Marijana Blažića 2
Tel: 320-320
www.hilton.com
150 rooms. € 250
Dubrovnik's first purpose-built hotel, funded in 1895 by a team of doctors who advocated sea bathing. Recently taken over and renovated by the Hilton chain, the Imperial offers everything a luxury hotel should offer, though it has no private beach.

LAPAD *Map p. 154*
Lapadska obala 37
Tel: 432-922
www.hotel-lapad.hr
300 rooms. € 40–100
Housed in a graceful former summer villa, with disused private chapel. The old stairway remains, otherwise the interior is cheap 'n' cheerless modern decor. Rooms are basic, but the location on the bay of Lapad, overlooking Gruž, is a pretty one.

View of Pile, with the Hotel Imperial.

NEPTUNE *Map p. 154*
Lapad, peninsula, Kardinala Stepinca 31
Tel: 440-100
www.hotel-neptun.hr
146 rooms. € 100/person
Modern hotel on the seafront on
the Lapad peninsula, linked to the
old town by a good bus route.
Comfortable and unexceptional but
a good choice for a beach holiday
with children.

PALACE *Map p. 154*
*Lapad peninsula, Masarykov put
20*
Tel: 430-194
www.dubrovnikpalace.hr
308 rooms. € 69–220/person
Self-contained hotel and spa
complex at the end of a regular
bus route (No. 4) from the old
town. Lots of grey slate and
faux rosewood—a strange
contrast to the pinewoods and
limestone outside the plate
glass. But for a lazy summer
lolling by the pool or jacuzzi
with teenagers, this could be
ideal.

PUCIĆ PALACE *Map p. 199, D4*
Od Puča 1.
Tel: 326-222
www.thepucicpalace.com
19 rooms and suites. € 400
Graceful town house, once the
residence of the Pucić family,
completely remodelled inside as a
luxurious hotel. Unbeatable location
inside the old city walls, right on the
main market square.

STARI GRAD *Map p. 198, C2*
Od Sigurate 4.
Tel: 322-244
www.hotelstarigrad.com
8 rooms. € 130
Sweet little hotel, once a patrician

town house, inside the old city walls. Rooms are simply furnished, and there is an upper terrace with panoramic views. Breakfast is offered in the downstairs café.

VILLA DUBROVNIK *Map p. 134, E*
Vlaha Bukovca 6
Tel: 422-933
www.laus.hr/villa-dubrovnik

40 rooms.   € 220–280 (€ 30 supplement for half-board)
Regular launch to the old port.
Much the nicest and most intimate of the modern hotels, with a beautiful terrace restaurant overlooking the old town. Situated a little further out than the others, it takes about 15 minutes to walk into the old town (quicker by the hotel boat). Excellent restaurant.

PRIVATE ACCOMMODATION

There are a number of private rooms offered in the old town and just outside it, many of which have self-catering facilities. General information can be obtained from the Dubrovnik Tourist Board at Cvijete Zuzorić 1 (*map p. 198, D3*). *Tel: 324-999. www.visitdubrovnik.hr*

The following websites also have lists and online booking:
www.dubrovnik-online.com
www.dubrovnik-apartments.com
www. apartments-dubrovnik.com
www. dubrovnik-reception.com

The main agencies handling accommodation are:

ATLAS
Ćira Carića 3 (main office)
Tel: 442-222; 442-855 (call centre)
www.atlas-croatia.com

GENERALTURIST
Obala Stjepana Radića 24
Tel: 432-937
www.generalturist.com

ELITE TRAVEL
Vukovarska 17
Tel: 358-200
www.elite.hr

PRACTICAL TIPS

CULTURAL FESTIVALS

ST BLAISE'S DAY: The feast day of St Blaise (Sveti Vlaho), February 3rd, is a day when the whole of Dubrovnik turns out to celebrate. Formerly, during the days of the Ragusan Republic, outlawed criminals could come to town without fear of conviction on St Blaise's Day itself, as well as the day before and the day after. Today the celebrations begin the day before, when two *festanjuli* ('feast hosts') are elected, one from among the local sea captains and the other from among the craftsmen. The *festanjuli* then travel to all the neighbouring parishes to invite people to the feast. Everyone arrives dressed in national costume and carrying their local village banners. The main St Blaise's Day procession attracts crowds of thousands as the saint's relics are paraded around the town, ending up at St Blaise's church. The Admiral of the Dubrovnik fleet, clad from head to foot in scarlet damask, used to proclaim 'Long life and victory, peace and prosperity, to this most serene and exalted Republic of Dubrovnik. May God protect her and keep her for many years on land and on sea!' Today the bishop blesses the city and its people, releasing three white doves.

THE SUMMER FESTIVAL: Every year between July 10th and August 25th Dubrovnik turns itself into a stage set. People from all over Croatia and beyond flock to the city, and international performing artists fly in to rub shoulders with the local talent. Open-air concerts and theatre performances are held at venues across the old town. Two traditions of the summer festival have now become inextricably part and parcel of the event. One is a performance of *Hamlet* in Fort Lovrijenac—a particularly effective setting for the ghost scene, which normally sends shivers up the audience's collective spine. The other is the declaiming of Ivan Gundulić's *Ode to Liberty*: *'Oh beautiful, oh sweet and precious liberty, The gift wherein our God-given wealth resides, The true foundation of our glory, Sole ornament of this city—All the silver in the world, all the gold and all human life can never pay for your pure beauty!'* Dubrovnik's long centuries of independence have made the city an important symbol of Croatian self-determination, and these stirring lines always bring a flutter to all patriotic Croatian hearts, giving an emotional charge to the whole festival.

Crowds throng the Stradun on February 3rd.

Information & Maps

The information office at the head of the Stradun (*map p. 198, C3*) has programmes of what's on and carries the free *Dubrovnik Riviera* and *In Dubrovnik* guides, which contain useful information and telephone numbers. Larger-scale maps of the greater Dubrovnik area are available from there too, as well as from most postcard and souvenir shops. Finding your way around the old town is incredibly easy after the first five minutes, and asking for directions can often be fruitless. Locals tend not to know the names of the streets, identifying them instead by a particular characteristic. Između Polača is better known as the bakery street, for example, because of its baker's shop Tanti Gusti.

Post Offices

There are three post offices in and near the old town: one on the corner of Široka and Đorđićeva (*map p. 198, C3*), one in Pile (*map p. 142, B3*), and another in Ploče (*map p. 134, A*).

Public Transport

Buses to Gruž leave regularly from Pile (bus Nos. 1A and 1B). Note that the front door has *ulaz* (entry) written on it in large letters, while *izlaz* (exit) is written on the others. You are supposed to take these instructions seriously, and drivers can get quite shirty with people who don't. If getting off the bus at the last stop, the rule no longer applies. Either buy your ticket direct from the driver or at the main Pile bus stop. A general ticket is valid for one hour.

Useful Bus Lines

1A, 1B: From Pile to Mokošica via Gruž and Rijeka Dubrovačka.

4: Pile to Lapad (Hotel Palace).

5: Ploče to Lapad (Hotel Neptune).

6: Pile to Lapad (Hotels Lapad, President, Neptune).

BEACHES

Dalmatians claim not to like sandy beaches, because the sand covers up their beautiful rocks. Around Dubrovnik, rocky beaches definitely predominate. Most hotels have private bathing. The best of the public beaches are:

BANJE: An expansive sweep just outside the Ploče gate. Beach chairs and curtained four-poster loungers for rent. The East West restaurant serves bar food and full meals, though you can't use the restaurant in swimsuit only. *Map p. 134, B.*

Banje beach.

LOKRUM: Swim from the rocks on the far side of the island, or on the more sheltered near side, facing the mainland, where the water is calmer and warmer. Watch out for sea urchins! *Map p. 154.*

SULIĆ: Small, protected pebbly cove, chiefly used for water polo, though locals like it for its clean swimming water too. Access through a low stone doorway on Od Tabakarije. *Map p. 142, B/C4.*

ŠUNJ: A sheltered sandy cove on the island of Lopud. The land shelves so shallowly that you can wade out for a long time before getting out of your depth, and the water is wonderfully warm. Nudists welcome. *Map p. 154.*

SV. JAKOV: Small sand-and-pebble cove with views back towards the old town. Accessible only down a long steep flight of steps (*see p. 139*) from behind the former monastery of St James, at the end of ulica Vlaha Bukovca. *Map p. 134, F.*

BOATS, FERRIES & BOAT HIRE

Ferries to the Elaphite Islands leave from the main port of Gruž. Timetables and tickets are available from the Jadrolinija office at Stjepana Radića 40 in Gruž, directly opposite the main quay. (*Open 8am–4.15pm & 7pm–8pm; Sun 8am–10am & 5pm–6.30pm.*) and you can also find out boat times from the information office on the Stradun, on the corner of Od Sigurate (*map p. 198, C3; Tel: 323-350*). Timetables are also printed in the free, widely available *Dubrovnik Riviera Guide* and in *In Dubrovnik*, another free guide.

Boats to Cavtat and Lokrum leave from Dubrovnik old harbour. Atlas can arrange boats of all sizes, motor launches, yacht charter, private day trips, in addition to a range of group bus and boat tours. *Lučarica 1, Tel: 324-745. atlas@atlas.hr; www.atlas-croatia.com*

For day trips to the islands, Trsteno, Zaton and Cavtat, Captain Žarko Knego can take you in his launch. *Tel: 417-232; mobile: 098 243 264.*

Sailing boats can also be hired from the ACI Marina at Rijeka Dubrovačka. *Tel: 455 020/1; Fax: 455 022. www.aci-club.hr*

Jeanneau motor boats and sailing boats can be chartered from Euromarine; *Tel: 451-465; www.euromarine.hr*

SELECT BIBLIOGRAPHY

English-language sources:

Bridge, Ann: *Illyrian Spring*. Chatto & Windus, 1935. Enjoyably dated novel about families learning to appreciate each other, with excellent architectural descriptions of Dubrovnik.
Brown, Ann: *Before Knossos... Arthur Evans's Travels in the Balkans and Crete*. University of Oxford, Ashmolean Museum, 1993.
Carter, Francis W: *Dubrovnik (Ragusa): A Classic City-state*. Seminar Press, London & New York, 1972.
Cuddon, J.A: *The Companion Guide to Jugoslavia*. Collins, London. 3rd revised edition, 1986.
Dračevac, Ante: *Dubrovnik Cathedral*. Privredni Vjesnik, Zagreb, 1988. Copies of this detailed guide are sold at the cathedral treasury.
Foretić, Miljenko, Ed: *Dubrovnik in War*, 6th edition. Matica hrvatska, Dubrovnik, 2000. A collection of essays, in various languages, about the events of 1991–92.
Frucht, Richard, Ed: *Encyclopedia of Eastern Europe*. Garland, New York & London, 2000.
Harris, Robin: *Dubrovnik: A History*. Saqi, London, 2003. Very readable scholarly history.
Krasić, Stjepan: *The Dominican Priory in Dubrovnik*. Dominikanski Samostan Sv. Dominika, Dubrovnik, 2002.
Margaritoni, Marko: *Dubrovnik: Between History & Legend*. Dubrovnik State Archives, 2001. Erratically translated but highly engaging collection of folk tales and legends about Dubrovnik and its environs.
Prosperov Novak, Slobodan: *Dubrovnik Revisited*. Biblioteka Ambrozia, Zagreb, 2005. History, anecdote and fascinating titbits about Ragusa past and present.
Singleton, Fred: *A Short History of the Yugoslav Peoples*. Cambridge University Press, 1985.
Tanner, Marcus: *Croatia: A Nation Forged in War*. Yale Nota Bene, 1997.
West, Rebecca: *Black Lamb & Grey Falcon*, vol. I. Macmillan & Co, London, 1942. Over-written, opinionated comment from one of the few people who didn't like what they saw when they came to Dubrovnik.
Whelpton, Eric: *Dalmatia*. Robert Hale, London, 1954.

INDEX

Numbers in italics refer to illustrations. Numbers in bold are major references.

A

Adriatic 13, 16, 27, 28, 30, 33
Aegean 15
Aesculapius 58, 171
Agricola, Emperor 11
Albania 15, 22, 100
America (*see United States*)
Amerling family 73, 112, 114, 144
Ancona 26, 136
Andreotti, Paolo 79
Andrijić family 66, 90, **94**, *94*, 104, 115
di Antivari (*see Brajkov*)
Antunini fraternity 84, 131
Armada (*see Spanish Armada*)
Armenia 11
Arsenal *48*, **49–50**
Atlantic 28
Augustus, Emperor 171
Austria, Austrian 19, 20, 21 22, 28, 29, 33,
        37, 42, 43, 55, 62, 84, 92, 127, 132,
        139, 146, 150, 151, 156
Austria-Hungary 21, 52, 84, 112, 144, 181
Avars 13, 171

B

Baldwin of Flanders 15
Balkan, Balkans 67, 68, 84
Banje beach (*see Beaches*)
Baroque architecture 68, 77, 79, 105
Bartolommeo, Maso di 72, 89
Basil I, Emperor 13
Beaches: Banje 136, 189, *189*; Lokrum 189,
        189; Sv. Jakov *138*, 139, 189; Sulić 189;
        Šunj 158–9, *158*, 189
Beccadelli, Lodovico 159–60
Belltower 52, 127
Benedictine monastery (*see Monasteries*)
Benedictines 72, 78, 102, 123, 152

Blaise, St **11**, *11*, *12*, 40, 43, 113; (*church of,
        see Churches*); (*festival*) 11, 80, **186**, *187*;
        (*relics of*) **80–81**, *80*, 186
Bogomils 102
Bokar, Fort (*see Fort Bokar*)
Bošković, Anica 69
Bošković, Ruđer 62, 80, **84**, *84*, 105
Bosnia, Bosnian 14, 16, 19, 24, 50, 61, 82,
        102, 135
Božidarević, Nikola *12*, 74, 75, *97*, **97–8**,
        146
Bremen 54
British 156
Brajkov, Mihoje 70
Brsalje **143ff**, *143*
Buda 18
Buffalini, Andrea 79
Bukovac, Vlaho 71, 74, **98–9**, **139**, *169*, 171
Bulgaria 14, 15, 22
Bunić, Nikolica **61**, *61*, 116
Bunićeva poljana 116
Buža gate 40, 129
Byron, Lord 167
Byzantium, Byzantine 9, 13, 14, 15, 26, 101,
        113; (*architecture*) 13, 78, **87**, 101, 104;
        (*art*) 75, 97

C

Cafés & Bars: Buža 180, *181*; Cele 180–1;
        Dubravka 144; Festival 131, *180*, 181;
        Gradska Kavana 50, 181, *181*; Karaka
        124; Troubador *116*
Catalans 7, 16
Cathedral (*see Churches*)
Catholic, Catholicism 14, 68, 84, 102, 159
Cavtat 13, 16, 32, 48, 58, 84, 96, 99, 100,
        170–1, *170*
Cerruti, Giulio 51

Charlemagne 53

Charles V, Holy Roman Emperor 28

Charlotte of Belgium 150

Christian, Christianity 13, 14, 18, 27, 28, 101, 102, 106

Churches and chapels: All Saints (*see Domino*); Annunciation 94; Cathedral **78ff**, *78*, *79*, 112; Dančе (*see Convents*); Dominican **74**, *74*, 93, 99, 160; Domino 121, 122; Franciscan **68–9**, *69*, 88, 89, 95; Holy Saviour (Sv. Spas) 53, 94, *94*, **103–4**; Jesuit **104–5**, *105*, 112; Holy Cross *153*, 158; Rosary 72, 128; St Blaise (Sv.Vlaho) 68, **76–7**, *76*, 91, 99, 186; St George (Sv. Đurđa) 144, *145*; St James (Sv. Jakov) 88, *88*; St James (Sv. Jakov Višnjica) *133*, 139; St Jerome 158; St Lazarus 79, 136; St Luke (Sv. Luka) *85*, 90; St Mary's (Lopud) 156; St Michael (Trsteno) 167, **168**, *168*; St Nicholas (Sv. Nikola) 128, *128*; St Peter (Sv. Petar) 87, *87*, 124; St Roch (Sv. Roka) 120, *120*; St Sebastian 72, 99; St Vitus 130; SS Cosmas & Damian *86*, 87, 115; St Stephen (Sv. Stjepan) 113, *113*; Serbian Orthodox **104**; Sigurata 131; Transfiguration (*see Sigurata*); Our Lady of the Snows (Cavtat) 96, 170, 171; Our Lady of Šunj 158–9; Visitation 147

Churchill, Winston 22

City Guard, headquarters of 128

City statute 15, 130

City walls (*see Walls*)

Clocktower *125*, 127

Communism, Communist 22

Constantinople 14, 40, 41, 49, 61, 81, 101, 102

Convents: Dančе 96, 98, 136, **145–6**, *146*, *147*; St Catherine of Siena 124; St Clare's 82, **102–3**, *103*, 119; St Mary's 119, 122–23, *122*; Sigurata 131

Croatia, Croatian 13, 16, 21, 22, 23, 26, 27, 84, 87, 132, 186

Crusades 14–15, 78, 150, 167

D

Dalmatia, Dalmatian 13, 17, 21, 22, 26, 29, 43, 55, 87, 90, 93, 96, 104, 132, 173

Dalmatinac, Juraj 41, 62, 93

Dančе (*see Convents*)

Della Cava, Onofrio 53, 57, 58, **93**, 120

Dobričević, Lovro 71, 75, *75*, **96**, *96*, 97, 146, *147*, 171

Doge of Venice 13, 14, 15, 26

Dominican church (*see Churches*)

Dominican friary **72ff**, *73* (plan), 89, *89*, 128

Dominican friary museum (*see Museums*)

Dominicans 68, 72, 88, 102

Drobac, Antun 130

Držić, Marin 59, 121, 121–2, **132**

Dubrovačka, river (*see Rijeka Dubrovačka, Ombla*)

Dubrovnik Commune 14, 15, 23, 34

Dubrovnik Statute (*see City Statute*)

Dulčić, Ivo 74, **77**, *98*, 99

Durbešić, Tomislav 51

E

Earthquakes: (1520) 24, 66, 103; (1667) 18, 23, **24**, 35, 53, 58, 61, 66, 68, 71, 76, 79, 81, 83, 86, 95, 104, 105, 106, 120, 129, 162; (1979) 24, 80, 115

Eastern Church 14, 101 (*see also Orthodoxy*)

Elaphite islands 13, 48, **155ff**

England, English 18, 28, 29, 139, 156, 159

Epidaurum 13, 58, 123, 171

Eugene of Savoy, Prince 18, 19

Evans, Arthur 42–3, 137

F

Festival, Summer (*see Summer Festival*)

Florence, Florentine 41, 58, 72, 83, 89, 93, 95

Forts: Bokar **42–3**, 93, *143*, 144, *173*; Imperial 41, Lovrijenac (*see Lovrijenac*); Revelin (*see Revelin*); Royal 139, 152; St John (Sv. Ivan) *8*, 43, 48, 92, 93, 100

France, French 20, 36, 62, 73, 98, 103, 122, 150, 152, 156

Francia, Francesco 71
Francis of Assisi, St 68, 71
Franciscan church (*see Churches*)
Franciscan friary **68ff**, *70*, *71*, 88
Franciscan friary museum (*see Museums*)
Franciscans 68, 72, 102, 131, 145
Franks, Frankish 14
Franz I, Emperor of Austria 157
Franz Joseph, Emperor 21, 30, 150, 151

G

Gaj, Ljudevit 132
García, Gaetano 105
Germany, Germans: 7, 16, 23, 96; (*in WW2*)
    22 (*see also Nazis*)
Getaldić, Marin 61, **84**, 137
Gothic architecture 43, 58, 59, 68, *69*, 72,
    73, 74, 88, 89, 94, 129, 157
Gozze (*see Gučetić*)
Gradac, Park 146–7
Gradić, Stjepan 79
Great Britain (*see Britain*)
Great Council 15, 34, 35, 36, 62, 65, 92,
    98, 167
Greece, Greeks 7, 13, 15, 16, 33, 104, 155,
    170
Gregory VII, Pope 101
Gregory XI, Pope 27
Grgić, Miljanko 174
Gropelli, Marino 68, 76
Gruž 11, 22, 30, 31, 48, **162**
Gučetić family **167**, 168
Gundulić, Ivan 69, 87, 105, 111, **112**, **132**,
    132, 186
Gundulićeva poljana 111–2, *111*, 132

H

Habsburgs 21, 84, 92, 137, 146, 150, 151
Hamzić, Mihajlo 64, *64*, 75, *95*, **96–7**
Harbour (*see Old port*)
Haydn, Joseph 140
Herzegovina 19, 43, 137
Holland 18, 29
Holy Land 28, 68

Holy Roman Empire/Emperor 14, 19, 28, 54
Hotels: Argentina 137, **183**; Excelsior 79,
    136, **183**, *183*; Hilton Imperial 68, 144,
    183; Lafodia 156; Lapad 183; Libertas
    145; Neptune 184; Palace 184–5;
    Pucić Palace 184; Sheherezade 137,
    137, 183; Stari Grad 184–5; Villa
    Dubrovnik 139, **185**; Villa Orsula 183
Hungary, Hungarian 16, 17, 18, 19, 21, 22,
    23, 27, 28, 82, 132

I

Illyrian Provinces 20, 54
Illyrians 13, 33, 34, 155
Islam 28 (*see also Muslim*)
Istanbul (*see Constantinople*)
Italy, Italian: 9, 16, 26, 34, 72, 95, 97, 132,
    139, 173, 180; (*artists in Dubrovnik*) 68,
    89, 94, 95, 104; (*in WW2*) 22, 44
Ivan, Fort Sv. (*see Forts, St John*)

J

Jesuit College 104, 105–6, 112
Jesuit church (*see Churches*)
Jesuit steps **92**, 104, 112
Jesuits 65, 84, **104–5**, 106, 112
Jews 9, 16, **106–7**, 129
Johnson, Samuel 84

K

Kaboga, Marojica **61**, 116
Kara Mustafa 61
Karađorđević family 22
Kaše *8*, 49, 93
Kolendić, Marko 75
Koločep 87, 156
Komolac 163, 164
Konavle 16, 132, 135
Korčula 58, 62, 66, 94, 140, 174
Kotor, Bay of 16
Kulin, Ban of Bosnia 102

L

Ladislas of Naples 17

Lastovo 15
Lauriston, General Alexandre 7, 40
Lazaretto (see *Quarantine Hospital*)
Leopold of Austria 19
Lepanto, Battle of 28
Levant 11, 131
Lokrum 11, *39*, 48, 72, 78, 102, 139, *149*, **150–2**, *151*, 189
Lopud 32, 75, **156–9**, *157*
Louis, King of Hungary 16, 17, 27
Lovrijenac, Fort 39, *43*, **44**, **144**, 186
Lovrin, Vicko **96**, 171
Lučić, Hannibal 130
Luža 50, 127–28

M

Mali Ston (see *Ston*)
Mali Zaton (see *Zaton*)
Maritime Museum (see *Museums*)
Martino, Pietro di 53, 58, 93
Marmont, Auguste Frédéric 20, 40, 64–65, 152, 167
Matejević, Petar 77
Matov, Jerolim 82
Matthias Corvinus, King 82
Maximilian, Archduke **150**, 151, 152
Medici family 58, 83, 93
Mediterranean 18, 22, 25, 28, 29, 30, 33, 40
Menčetić family 41
Meštrović, Ivan 32, 43, 74, **99**, *99*, 171
Mexico 150
Michelangelo 159, 160
Michelozzo 41, 42, *57*, **58**, 62, 93, **93**
Milan, Milanese 53, 75, 84
Milano, Bonino da 54
Miličević, Pasko 40, 43, 44, 49, 66, **93**, 94
Minčeta tower **41**, *41*, 93
Mohács, Battle of 18, 28
Monasteries: Benedictine (on Lokrum) 150–1, *151*; Dominican (see *Dominican friary*); Franciscan (see *Franciscan friary*); Franciscan (in Cavtat) 171; Franciscan (on Lopud) 156; Franciscan (Rožat) *161*, 164; St James (Sv. Jakov)

139
Mongols 136
Montenegro, Montenegrin 70, 164
Mosque **107**, 124
Museums: Bukovac 171; Dominican friary **74–5**, 96, 97, 98, 160; Držić 121, 132; Dulčić Masle Pulitika 100; Franciscan friary **71**, 96; Maritime 43, 99, **100**, 160; Modern art 100; Rector's Palace (see *Rector's Palace*); Rupe **100**, 122
Music School 124
Muslims 9, 61, 101, 102, 107, 135

N

Naples, Neapolitan 53, 93
Napoleon **20–21**, 23, 30, 36, 37, 40, 54, 64, 73, 122, 140, 150, 156, 164, 167
Napoleon III 150
Nazis 22, 107
Netherlands 28 (see also *Holland*)
Normans 14, 26
Nunneries (see *Convents*)

O

Od Puča 120–1
Od Pustijerne 86, 90, **111ff**.
Od Tabakarije 145
Old port **48–50**, *48*, *50*, 93
Ombla, river *162*, 163–4
Onofrian fountains *52*, 53, *53*, 71, *119*
Orlando's column **53–5**, *54*, 156
Orphanage, Dubrovnik 102–3, 119
Orseolo, Pietro 13
Orsini, Giorgio (see *Dalmatinac, Juraj*)
Ostoja, King of Bosnia 16
Orthodox church (see *Churches*)
Orthodoxy 84, 101, 102, 104
Ottoman: (*general*) 21, 28, 40, 65, 112; (*empire*) 17, 18, 36, 86; (*sultan*) 17, 28, 81 (see also *Turkey, Turkish*)

P

Padua 115
Pamotta, Giacomo 24

Paris 19, 99, 139, 171
Partisans 22
Pelješac 16, 168, 174
Peloponnese 15
Peter the Martyr, St 75, *75*
Petrović brothers 68, 89, 90
Pharmacy, Franciscan 71
Philip II, King of Spain 28
Pile: (*area*) 44, 72, **143ff**; (*gate*) 40, **43**, 52, 68, 99, 143
Placa (*see Stradun*)
Plague 41, 61, 70, 76, 106, 136
Ploče: (*area*) 72, **135ff**, *135*, 146; .(*gate*) 40, **43**, 53
Poland, Polish 132
Poljana Mrtvo Zvono 123
Porphyrogenitos, Constantine 113
Porporela 48, 92, *92*
Port, old (*see Old Port*)
Portugal, Portuguese 28
Pozzo, Andrea 105
Pracat, Miho 32, **59–60**, *60*, **157–8**, 159
Prague 99, 171
Preradović, Petar 21
Prijeko 86, *128*, 128–9, 130–1
Pucić family 75, 144, 147
Pulitika, Đuro 74, **99**, 130

Q
Quarantine 67
Quarantine hospital *8*, 136, 146

R
Račić: (*family*) 171; (*Ivo*) 32; (*mausoleum*) 32, 99, *99*, 171
Ragusan Commune (*see Dubrovnik Commune*)
Ragusano, Nicola (*see Božidarević*)
Ragusinus, Paulus 59
Ranjina family *90*, 115
Raphael *82*, 83
Rector of Dubrovnik 14, 17, 24, 34, 59, 62, 64, 65, 67, 79, 81, 85, 132
Rector's Palace *20*, *33*, **57ff**, *57*, *58*, *59*, 61,
63 (*plan*), *64*, 66, 89, 93, 97, 157
Renaissance architecture 18, 24, 43, 51, *57*, 58, 59, 66, 72, 89, 90, 93, 94, 114, *115*, 157, 160
Renaissance art 68, 97
Restaurants: Ankora 166, *166*; Antunini 131, 175, *175*; Dundo Maroje 175; East West 175, *177*; Kamenice 175–6; Lokanda Peskarija 176, *176*; Mea Culpa 176; Nautika 176–7; Orhan 144, *173*; Orsan 166; Penatur 177; Poklisar 50; Posat 177; Proto 177; Rozarij 128, 177; Sesame 147; Spaghetteria Toni 177; Taverna Rustica 136, *136*
Revelin 40, 43, 135
Richard I, King of England 78, 150
Rijeka Dubrovačka 53, *161*, *162*, *163*, **163–4**
Roland (*see Orlando*)
Romanesque architecture 68, 70, 78, **88**, *88*
Romania 22
Rome, Roman 19, 51, 79, 82, 84, 92, 93, 105, 112, 159; (*ancient*) 9, 11, 13, 33, 34, 155, 170
Roosevelt 22
Rožat (*see Monasteries*)
Rudolf, Crown Prince 151
Rupe (*see Museums*)
Russia, Russian 20, 30, 40, 61, 164

S
Sagroević, Nikola 25
St Clare's Convent (*see Convents*)
St John (*see Forts, St John*)
St Mary's Convent (*see Convents*)
Salona 13
Saracens 9, 26, 35, 53, 54
Saraka family 137
Senate of Dubrovnik 15, 20, 24, 34, 36, 40, 57, 67, 79, 81, 112, 123
Serbia, Serbs 15, 16, 23, 84, 104
Serbs, Croats and Slovenes, Kingdom of 21, 23
Sheherezade 137, *137*, 139
Sicily 26

Siege of Dubrovnik 22–23, 53, 55 (see also
    Wars, with Serbia)
Sigismund, King of Hungary 27
Šipan 32, **159–60**, *159*
Skočibuha: (summer residence) 160; (town
    residence) 90, 94, **114–5**, *115*, 160;
    (Tomo) 32, 160; (Vice) 32, 36, *36*, 90,
    160
Slaves, slave-trade 26, 102
Slavonia, Slavonic 13, 132, 150, 171
Slavs, Slavic 10, 13, 16, 21, 34, 39, 52, 84,
    101, 102, 128, 132, 155, 171
Small Council 15, 34, 98
Sorkočević: (Antun) 140; (family) 115, 163;
    (Luka) 115, 124, **140**
Spain 28, 106
Spanish Armada 28, 160
Split 29
Sponza Palace 51, **66–7**, *66*, *67*, 90, 93–4,
    94, 127
Srđ, Mt 9, 41, 52, 101
Stalin, Joseph 22
Stoico, Canon 11, 113
Ston 15, 16, 93, **168**
Stradun 13, **51ff**, *51*, *56*, 68, 71, 86, 91,
    128, 144, 170
Strossmayer, Bishop **84**, 104, 150–1, 171
Summer Festival 44, 55, 59, 67, **186**
Šunj: beach (see Beaches); church (see
    Churches)
Supilo, Frano 21, **84**
Sv. Andrija, island 32, 136, 156
Sv. Ivan (see Forts, St John)
Sv. Spas (see Churches, Holy Saviour)
Synagogue **106–7**, *107*, 129

T
Tasso, Torquato 62, 166
Theatre, Marin Držić 49, 116
Titian 75, 79–80, 95, 167, 168, *168*
Tito 22
Town Hall 65, 92
Transfiguration, Church of (see Churches,
    Sigurata)

Trsteno *165*, **167**, *167*
Turkey, Turks 17, 18, 19, 20, 23, 28, 29,
    40, 43, 50, 61, 132, 180 (see also
    Ottoman)

U
United States 22, 23, 99, 139
Urbino 79

V
Varna 17
Veliki Ston (see Ston)
Veneziano, Paolo 74
Venetian Gothic architecture 57, 58, 66, *66*,
    71, 89, 90, 115
Venice, Venetian 9, 11, 13, 14, **14–15**, 16,
    17, 18, 20, 23, 26, **26–7**, 28, 29, 30,
    34, 49, 76, 80, 86, 91, 104, 112, 113,
    121, 132
Vienna 18, 19, 30, 61, 84, 105, 137, 151
Vienna, Congress of 21, 23, 37, 55
Visconti family 158
Vlaho, Sv. (see Blaise, St)
Vojnović, Ivo 40

W
Walls, around old town **39ff**, *39*, *42* (plan),
    58
Wars: (with Serbia) 22–23, 112, 145, 181
    (see also Siege of Dubrovnik); (World
    War One) 21; (World War Two) 22, 34,
    44, 67
Watkins, Thomas 85
Whelpton, Eric 33

Y
Yugo wind 123
Yugoslavia 21, 22, 23, 30, 84

Z
Zagreb 19, 132
Zaton 166, *166*
Žudioska, ulica 106, 129, *129*
Zuzorić, Cvijeta 62, 166

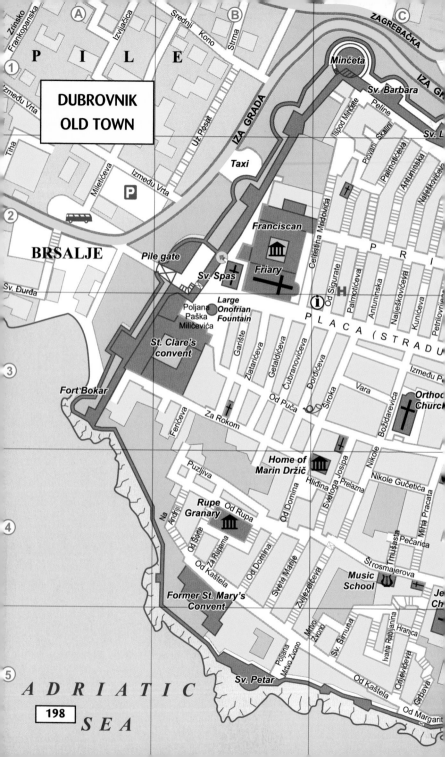

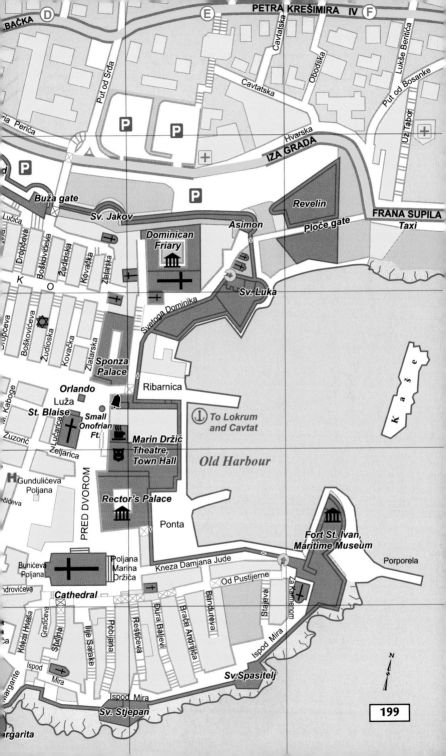

SOMERSET BOOKS
Blue Guides Limited,
Registered office: Winchester House, Dean Gate Avenue,
Taunton TA1 2UH, England
Repro studio: *Timp Kft.*
Printed in Hungary by: *Dürer Nyomda Kft.*
ISBN 1-905131-15-1